Michael and Rita Little

Collins
Glasgow and London

We dedicate this book to:
Kevin, Becky and Glen

Maps of France and introductory route maps
Rita Little

Strip maps
Reg and Marjorie Piggott

First published 1985
Revised edition 1986
Copyright © Michael and Rita Little 1985
Copyright © strip maps Wm. Collins Sons & Co. Ltd.
Published by William Collins Sons and Company Limited
Printed in Great Britain

ISBN 0 00 447477 5

Foreword

We cannot tell you how delighted we are that Collins decided to produce a second edition of *France Coast to Côte*. Even more pleasing has been the response we have received from those readers who successfully followed our routes through France.

We particularly enjoyed the wonderful sense of humour of one poor chap who due to mechanical problems failed to get beyond Calais. He wrote to us saying that our book had been of immense help so far.

Your letters, comments and criticism have been an invaluable aid to updating the book. We must also confess to having enjoyed the role of minor celebrities even if it was only at our local pub.

Several people have complained that all our routes serve those on the outward journey and have asked why we did not produce separate ones for the run home. It is quite easy to follow our routes backwards, all you need to do is take care in some towns where one-way systems may make minor changes to the path you follow.

When preparing a route from the UK into France it is never difficult to describe the starting place, quite obviously it is the point where you drive off the ferry. Return routes are rather a different matter for everyone wants to start from a different place in France. Nevertheless, in this new edition we have produced one homeward-bound route which will certainly appeal to those looking for a leisurely run up through France. It is the Route Napoléon. We follow closely the line used by the Emperor when he returned from the island of Elba in 1815.

We have chosen the Boulevard d'Alsace as the starting point because it is not difficult to locate. This is the expressway which runs through the centre of Cannes. In fact, Napoléon landed a few miles down the coast at Golfe-Juan.

The Route Napoléon was constructed in the early 1930s through terrain which had previously been impossible to negotiate by wheeled vehicle. Apart from the last few kilometres into Grenoble it is shown on your map as the RN85.

Napoléon covered the 200 miles to Grenoble in six days, part by coach but mostly on horseback. His soldiers followed on foot. Our research trip involved covering several parts of the route more than once, and we frequently took diversions to follow more closely the actual route taken by Napoléon. We took six and a half days to cover the route (Napoléon 1 — Michael & Rita 0). We have a strange feeling that it cost us more as well.

Throughout its length the Route Napoléon is marked with the sign of an eagle which you will see at the entrance and exit of each village and town. This was Napoléon's personal emblem. During his famous march he repeatedly stated 'The eagle will fly from steeple to steeple until it reaches the towers of Notre Dame.'

Those following the route should not take lightly our statement that it is a leisurely way home. Two full days driving must be allowed to cover the run from Cannes to Tournus, a distance which can quite easily be driven on the motorway in five hours. At Tournus we link into the A6 or N6 (our routes Five or Twelve). So please remember the Route Napoléon is not a route for those in haste for although the road is mostly up to RN standard it is in parts mountainous and tortuous. Also this is a road to be used only in summer months as it is subject to heavy snow and it is not uncommon for the passes to be closed between November and April.

Bon route
Michael and Rita Little

Contents

1

The maps contained in this book are diagrammatic route finders. The scale has been altered to enable you to see each stage of your route clearly.

The maps have been specially drawn to match the accompanying text. Distances are given in km (**58**km) between the towns marked with a flag symbol ⚑

We recommend that the book be used in conjunction with the red Michelin map of France, no. 989 (1cm:10km). This map is readily available in the UK from all good booksellers. Those who prefer maps in book form can purchase Collins Road Atlas of Europe which is equally suitable for use with this book and has the advantage that it also covers the UK.

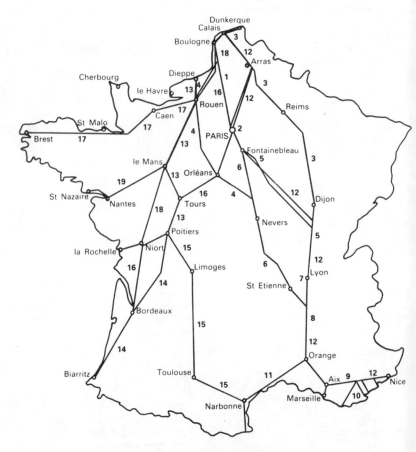

Contents

2

South of France

South West France and the Dordogne

Normandy, Brittany and the Loire Valley

Errata

The route and maps on pp 101 — 104 is Route Fifteen, not Route Sixteen as is stated incorrectly on the headings of these four pages.

Planning Your Holiday

Selecting Your Route

An ideal way to enjoy your holiday journeys is to drive out by one route and return by another. All the routes may be used in the opposite direction simply by reversing the directions and maps. Some care will be necessary where one-way systems affect the flow of traffic in towns.

The South of France Routes One to Twelve take you from the Channel ports of Calais or Boulogne through the centre of France — Paris and Lyon can be avoided by those who dislike driving in big cities. From the centre of France all routes converge on the Rhône Valley, passing between two mountain ranges, the Alpes to the east and the Massif Central to the west. Experience has shown us that this is the best way to reach the Mediterranean as you can avoid the mountain roads.

If you want to reach your destination as quickly as possible, Route Twelve or the combination of Routes Twelve and Eleven take you almost the total distance from the French Channel ports to the Mediterranean

by motorway. These routes are less interesting than the others and you will have to pay tolls but you will get there in the shortest time.

When driving to the south of France it is not necessary to follow any single one of our routes from start to finish.

For example, the combination of routes we prefer when driving to the Côte d'Azur is:

Route One from Calais or Boulogne to Paris picking up
Route Two around Paris to Fontainebleau. Then on to
Route Five to Lyon.
Route Seven is the Lyon bypass system. From Lyon we follow
Route Eight to a point just south of Valence where we join
Route Twelve to bypass Montélimar, Orange and Avignon. Then it is
Route Nine to our destination.

When driving right through France you may prefer to avoid Paris. Take our Route Three via Reims to Lyon

Those who really dislike driving in large towns may well favour Route Four which leads into Route Six, making it easy to bypass both Paris and Lyon

South-West France and the Dordogne
Routes Thirteen and Fourteen take you
across the Loire Valley on to Bordeaux and
Biarritz. Route Sixteen takes you direct
from Calais to Bordeaux by motorway.
Routes Thirteen and Fifteen go via the
Dordogne to Narbonne in Languedoc -

Roussillon. You can also reach Narbonne by
following the combination of Routes One,
Two, Five, Eight and Eleven.

This is a good example of how to see
more of the country. You can go out
by one set of routes and come home
by the other.

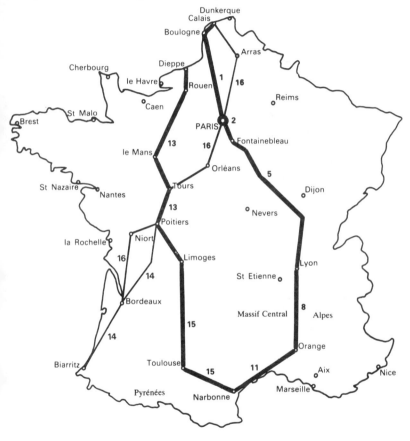

Normandy, Brittany and the Loire Valley If you plan to spend a holiday in Normandy or Brittany, you are well-blessed with a choice of ferry services which will deliver you to a point on the French coast quite close to your destination. When travelling to this part of France we like to cross from Newhaven to Dieppe.

Route Seventeen goes to Brest in the far west of Brittany and gives you the choice of taking detours to the Normandy Beaches, Mont-St-Michel or St Malo. Route Eighteen goes from Dunkerque, Calais or Boulogne to la Rochelle on the Atlantic coast. Route Nineteen takes you to St Nazaire on the coast via the Loire Valley.

Which Ferry

Before deciding which ferry company to use it is necessary to select the port of exit most convenient for your purpose.

If you live in the north of England or Scotland and you enjoy long sea crossings there is a case for choosing the Hull — Zeebrugge or Hook of Holland route. This means that you avoid a long drive on home soil. And if you take a cabin you can put a large slice of the journey behind you while you sleep.

If you come from East Anglia you may well prefer to head for Felixstowe, cross to Belgium or Holland and then head south into France on continental roads instead of driving a similar distance in the UK.

Those who live in the west country or Wales may prefer to cross from Portsmouth to Le Havre or Cherbourg, spending a night on the boat. If you live in southern England the Newhaven — Dieppe route is quite attractive and it avoids a hard drive in the wrong direction to reach Dover.

As long as you are a good sailor and the others in your party also enjoy life on board, it can be very pleasant to start and finish your holiday with a mini-cruise by ferry.

If you do not enjoy long sea crossings or live elsewhere then why not go via Dover which gives you a choice of two ferry firms plus the Hovercraft. Dover — Calais is the shortest crossing, lasting only 1 hour 30 minutes, while even better times are claimed by some of the newer vessels. Dover to Boulogne is only a few minutes longer, and the Hovercraft will rush you across to either Calais or Boulogne in about thirty-five minutes.

It would be unfair to ignore Folkestone and Ramsgate, both of which also offer comparatively short crossings. We must confess to a soft spot for Folkestone where we have found port officials, customs officers and immigration officials to have reliably good manners. Ramsgate seems to be the centre of a perpetual building site. When a new terminal does emerge from the confusion to grace the shores of Thanet it will surely only be as a consolation for the indignity of suffering a reception at Dunkerque in a wilderness of tarmac and Portakabins.

It is well worth while taking some time over selecting which ferry to use. The choice is not quite so straightforward as it at first appears.

For example, going south towards Paris: the Dover — Boulogne ferry crossing takes only a few minutes longer than the crossing to Calais. Those crossing to Boulogne, however, will start their journey through France some 34km/21mi nearer Paris, a very useful saving indeed.

If you cross to Calais and decide against using the toll motorways you have to drive that 34km/21mi of boring road before you pass through Boulogne.

However, the facilities offered to passengers at Boulogne fall far below those offered by the superb new ferry terminal at Calais. While we find the reception at Boulogne decidedly lacklustre, at Calais there is a very different atmosphere and you can sense the eagerness to be helpful.

At present Dunkerque is the only French Channel port linked through to Paris by motorway. This motorway, however, is probably of most use to drivers heading for Holland, Germany and Austria.

There is no hard and fast rule. It all depends on where you live, where you prefer to land in France and whether you enjoy sea crossings. When you have made the crossing a few times you will soon decide which is your favourite passage and which your favourite ferry operator.

Brochures containing information about each of the services may be obtained from the addresses on pp. 14-15 or from your local travel agent.

Booking Ferry Tickets When you have selected your route and you know which of the crossings suits you best you will, of course, require a ticket. Our advice is to book your outward journey in advance, reserving a place on the boat for your vehicle. Book your homeward passage on an open return basis which gives you the freedom of getting to a French Channel port in your own time and at your own pace. The ferry company then puts you on board the first sailing with space available. It costs no more to have this valuable flexibility.

At the end of a holiday a race back to Calais to catch a ferry is something well worth avoiding. Drivers who have covered hundreds of miles, rushing to catch a boat they imagine sailing without them, cannot perform at their best. It is possibly one of the main factors contributing to the high accident rate of homeward bound British motorists.

If you are travelling with a caravan or trailer in July or August it is essential to book your crossing both ways as space for caravans is not so readily available.

Out of high season it is often possible to arrive at Dover, buy your ticket on the spot and drive on board the next sailing. Not advised in peak holiday periods. A wait of several hours on British soil is frustrating as you watch others setting off for France.

We strongly advise that wherever possible you avoid Channel crossings on Saturdays. To help keep down the costs of cross-Channel ferry services the operators have built up a most disagreeable 'French Streaker' trade: on each Saturday throughout the year the normally tranquil ships suffer an invasion of day trippers who turn the decks, lounges, shops and bars into a milling Rovers Return.

Most of the French streaker shoppers travel on a day return basis. That is to say they travel outwards from the UK in the morning and return in the late afternoon or evening. If you are clever — you are — then you will plan your travel in such a way that you pass the hordes in mid-Channel as they go in the opposite direction.

Ferry Services to France

PORT	OPERATOR	SERVING	PASSAGE TIME
Plymouth	Brittany Ferries	Roscoff	6hrs
Weymouth	Sealink	Cherbourg	4 hrs 15 mins
Portsmouth	Sealink	Cherbourg	4 hrs 45 mins
Portsmouth	Brittany Ferries	St Malo	9 hrs
Portsmouth	Townsend Thoresen	Cherbourg	4 hrs 45 mins
Portsmouth	Townsend Thoresen	le Havre	5 hrs 30 mins
Portsmouth (from June '86)	Townsend Thoresen	Caen	5 hrs 30 mins
Newhaven	Sealink/Dieppe Ferries	Dieppe	4 hrs 15 mins
Folkestone	Sealink	Boulogne	1 hr 50 mins
Dover	Townsend Thoresen	Calais	1 hr 15 mins
Dover	Sealink	Dunkerque	2 hrs 20 mins
Dover	Sealink	Calais	1 hr 30 mins
Dover (Sats only)	Sealink	Boulogne	1 hr 40 mins
Dover	Townsend Thoresen	Boulogne	1 hr 40 mins
Dover	Hoverspeed	Calais	35 mins
Dover	Hoverspeed	Boulogne	35 mins
Ramsgate	Sally Line	Dunkerque	2 hrs 30 mins

Hovercraft and Ferry Operators

Brittany Ferries
Millbay Docks
Plymouth PL1 3EW
Tel: 0752 21321
French Tel: St Malo (99) 56-68-40
Roscoff (98) 68-22-11

Hoverspeed Ltd.
Maybrook House
Queen's Gardens
Dover
Kent CT17 9UQ
Tel: 01 554 7061
    0304 214514
French Tel: Calais (21) 96-67-10
Boulogne (21) 30-27-26

Sally Line Ltd.
54 Harbour Parade
Ramsgate
Kent
Tel: 01 858 1127
    0843 595522
Telex: 291860
French Tel: Dunkerque (28) 68-43-44

Sealink UK Ltd.
P.O. Box 29
Victoria Station
London SW1V 1JX
Tel: 01 834 8122
French Tel: Calais (21) 96-70-70
    Boulogne (21) 30-25-11
    Dieppe (35) 84-22-60
    Dunkerque (28) 66-80-01

Townsend Thoresen
127 Regent Street
London W1R 8LB
Tel: 01 734 4431
French Tel: Calais (21) 34-41-90
    Calais (21) 97-21-21
    le Havre (35) 21-36-50
    Cherbourg (33) 44-20-13
    Paris (1) 261 51-75

Arranging Accommodation

Whether you plan an overnight stop or a longer stay, the French Government Tourist Office at 178 Piccadilly, London W1, will be pleased to send you details of hotels and camp sites in the area you specify.

You can write off for a firm booking in English but say that you will be happy to receive the reply in French. This will speed up the response and you can translate their reply at leisure. (Sample letters on pp. 16 and 17 show how to reserve hotel accommodation or camping and caravan sites in French.) When you receive a booking do not forget to write and confirm it.

Renting a Villa The French tourist office (address above) will supply you with the address of the *syndicat d'initiative* (tourist office) in the main town of the area you wish to visit. If you write to them, in English, asking for a list of local people with

villas for rent, you may well be pleasantly surprised. It is certainly possible to rent direct from French owners at much lower rates than those offered by absentee British owners. Renting a villa or an apartment is a very economical way of accommodating a party of five people or more. One-room flatlets are also available. Very often renting bricks and mortar can be as cheap as renting a mobile home on a camp site.
Côte d'Azur If you plan a seaside holiday to the Côte d'Azur in season, from mid-June to mid-September, it is important that you make reservations in advance. If you are taking your own caravan you will be very, very lucky to find a site close to the Mediterranean unless you have booked and preferably paid a deposit in advance. One August night it was recorded that over 1000 caravans were without official sites, parked throughout Var in lay-bys and on grass verges, subject to being moved on by the Gendarmerie at any hour of the night. Unless you are prepared to accept a site miles from the sea, you must book in advance.

The French authorities are expanding the *Camping à la Ferme* system and several new sites are licensed each year. It is now much easier to find sites in May, June and September and we are informed that by 1988 there should be no problem in July and August.

It is also best to book hotel accommodation in advance as there is a serious shortage of rooms in July and August. However, if there are just two of you and you require only one room, you could just strike lucky. Never leave the search for a hotel room until after 6pm. The earlier in the day you enquire, the easier it will be to find a room. If your party is larger or you require more than one room you would be well advised to book before leaving home.
Provence It is possible to enjoy a wonderful holiday in Provence without going near the sea at all. There are beautiful lakes where you can swim, sail or windsurf and most towns have a good swimming pool. The weather is usually a few degrees warmer at a point 16km/10mi inland. There is no sea breeze — super hot!

SAMPLE LETTER (1)

The following wording suggested by the French Government Tourist Office may be found helpful when writing to reserve hotel accommodation in France.

Date

The Manager ....

Hotel ....

Address..

Town..

Monsieur le Directeur,
Dear Sir,

> *Je vous serais obligé de me communiquer*
> I should be grateful if you would let me know at

rapidement vos conditions et tarifs pour un séjour de ....nuits.
your earliest convenience your terms for staying........................nights.

> *commençant le .... à .... heures*   se terminant le.............. à .... heures**
> commencing .... at .... hours*   ending .... at .... hours*
> **(Please use the 24 hour clock)*

Nous sommes .... adultes et.................... enfants
We are.................................. adults and ....children

(.......................*filles âgées de*..............)   (.......................*garçons âgés de*............)
(.......................girls aged ....)   (.......................boys aged....................)

Nous souhaiterions réserver:
We would like to reserve:

.... *chambres à 2 lits (avec WC/bain/douche)*
..................twin bedded rooms (with WC/bath/shower)

.... *chambres à grand lit (avec WC/bain/douche)*
.... double rooms (with WC/bath/shower)

.... *chambres à un lit (avec WC/bain/douche)*
..............................single rooms (withWC/bath/shower)

Nous préférons pour les enfants .... chambres séparées (avec WC/bain/douche)
For the children we would prefer............ separate rooms (with WC/bath/shower)

Nous désirons la pension complète/demi-pension/la chambre et le petit déjeuner.
We would like to have full board/half board (bed, breakfast and one meal)/bed and breakfast.

> *Avec mes remerciements,*
> Yours faithfully,

Name ....

Address..

....

SAMPLE LETTER (2)

The following wording suggested by the French Government Tourist Office may be found helpful when writing to reserve camping and caravan sites in France.

Date

Monsieur le Directeur
Camping...
at..

Monsieur le Directeur,
Dear Sir,

       Je vous serais obligé de me communiquer rapidement vos conditions et tarifs
       I should be grateful if you would let me know at your earliest convenience

correspondant au séjour suivant:
your conditions for the following stay:

  Arrivée le ....   *Départ le*..
  Arriving on ....   Departing on ....

  Nous sommes .... *adultes et*....................*enfants agés de* .... *ans*
  We are ....adults and ....children aged .... years

  Nous désirons reserver un emplacement pour une voiture★ — tent★ — caravane★ —
  We wish to book a pitch for a car★ — tent★ — caravan★

caravane motorisée★ *louer une tente★ — caravane★ — bungalow★*
motor caravan★   hire a tent★ — caravan★ — bungalow★
                                        (★ delete where not applicable)

Veuillez me répondre directement à l'adresse ci-dessous:
Please answer direct to my address below:

  Mr./Mrs. ....

         ....

         ....
                     (block capitals please)
                       Avec mes remerciements,
                       Yours faithfully,

Preparing Your Vehicle

A Frenchman once told us he could spot a British car a mile away. 'It is the one with the roof rack.'

The average family saloon, with seats to spare most of the year, never seems large enough to take four people and their luggage on holiday. If it is to be a camping holiday some form of outside stowage will probably be required, and a roof rack is often the only answer to the problem.

Your car is likely to be subjected to more strain in two weeks than it endures the rest of the year. You will probably overload it and then drive it further and possibly faster than you would admit to your friends. Add a loaded roof rack and you will further upset the centre of gravity and distort the drag factors to the point where the designer's streamlined airflow no longer exists.

It is necessary to prepare your car for the punishment you intend to inflict upon it.

Checklist: Car Preparation

1. The vehicle should be given a full service.
2. All oils must be changed. (As engine oil is more expensive in France, it is a good idea to take some with you if your car tends to use oil. The smallest measure sold in France is a 2-litre can.)
3. Check tyres and replace if in the slightest doubt.
4. Examine spare tyre to make sure that the tread meets legal requirements, that it is correctly inflated and not too difficult to reach when the car is loaded.
5. Different tyre pressures are required on a heavily laden car.
6. It is not compulsory to fit yellow bulbs or lamp covers, but it costs very little to buy a small bottle of lamp glass paint to convert your existing lens to yellow. The French will appreciate your courtesy and it takes only seconds to wipe it off with methylated spirits when you return home.
7. Carefully mask the headlamp beam with small pieces of black sticky tape to direct your beam away from oncoming traffic in France. This method of beam redirection has the advantage that it is quickly removable should you arrive back in the UK with night driving in front of you.
8. Make sure your tool kit is accessible.
9. Fit a GB plate to rear of car and any trailer you may take with you.
10. Check your car thoroughly for any loose nuts or bolts.

Packing the Car Advance preparation saves frustration, time and money. It is a good idea to make out a checklist, ticking off each item as you pack the car. The following headings may be found useful when preparing your list.

REQUIRED EN ROUTE: overnight stay, tools, picnics (an economical way of eating en route is to pack a small basket with knives, forks, spoons, bottle opener, tin opener, corkscrew, paper plates, cups, etc., plus a few tins of meat or fish – when you arrive

in France your picnic is complete with the addition of French bread).

CLOTHES: Give this a lot of thought. Most people take far more clothing than they really require. However, it is unwise not to pack a sweater or two; late evening temperatures can be quite cool, even in July and August.

FOOD: Although food is generally lower in price and higher in quality in the bigger French supermarkets, there are two reasons for taking some food from home if you are going on a self-catering holiday: it can be fun putting together a holiday hamper and it allows you to spread the cost over a period; if you have children they may refuse to budge from the brands they know. (If you or the children like baked beans so much that you could not get through a holiday without them, take some tins with you. The French product is very different from the British equivalent.)

DRINK: In the unaccustomed heat children can consume huge quantities of soft drink. It is a good idea to take a one-gallon plastic container of orange squash concentrate. If you enjoy your cuppa do take your own teabags. The French product rarely suits British tastes.

ENTERTAINMENT: cards, games, books, etc.
BEACH REQUISITES: see p. 36.

Bear in mind that any item forgotten will have to be purchased out of your holiday fund and that every unnecessary item you carry with you will put an extra burden on your overworked car.

Checklist: Take With You In The Car

1. Passport and a valid driving licence. (Required by law)
2. The registration document of the vehicle. If you are not the registered owner you should obtain a letter giving you authority to take the vehicle out of the UK. (Required by law)
3. Insurance cover note and Green Card if you have obtained one. See separate section on Insurance p. 20. (Required by law)
4. Complete set of spare bulbs to fit every exterior and interior light on your vehicle. (Required by law)
5. You will need to carry a warning triangle to place in the roadway in the event of

breakdown or accident. (Required by law)

It is also common continental practice to raise the bonnet and the boot lid of a stationary vehicle to make it more conspicuous. Many motorists now paint the underside of bonnet and boot lid with fluorescent paint.

6. Carry a comprehensive tool kit. Even if you are not mechanically minded a stranger may help you if you have the tools. Add to your tool kit a roll of tape, a length of light electrical cable, a roll of wire and a selection of nuts, bolts, washers and self-tapping screws. *Do not forget a torch.*

7. It is a good idea to take a tow rope. It might help you get to a garage in the event of a breakdown. We once met an Englishman whose car had died beside a French autoroute. He tied his tow rope to the front of the car and held it in one hand while he thumbed a lift with the other. The French seemed suitably amused. It took fourteen separate tows to get from Auxerre to Calais where he pushed his car onto the boat. What a holiday.

8. Make sure you have adequate maps. The red Michelin map of France, no. 989 (1cm : 10km), will probably meet all your requirements. If you want a more detailed map of any particular area, the yellow Michelin series is on a scale of 1cm : 2 km.

Both are readily available in the UK.

9. If you are travelling with children take things to amuse them during the journey. A good supply of pads of paper, pencils and crayons and card games are usual favourites. Do not give them these items when you leave home, wait until they become as bored and impossible as only your kids can.

10. Take with you those tablets, pills and bottles that you rely upon at home. It is not uncommon for holiday-makers to become ill. This is often caused not by a change of diet or different water, but by fatigue and excess sun. Fatigue is the main culprit. If you set out to drive further, swim further, walk further and eat and drink more than you would at home, you cannot really blame France if you become ill.

11. If you have no French, or your French is rusty, take a phrase book and dictionary with you. If you get into difficulty and are at a loss for words you can always point to the relevant phrase or word in the book. Collins French Phrase Book and Gem Dictionary are easy to carry and readily available.

12. Do not forget your tickets or any other vital piece of paper such as telephone numbers and addresses, traveller's cheques, etc., – all easily overlooked in the heat of departure.

Money Matters

Traveller's Cheques Although most banks in the UK can produce sterling traveller's cheques at a few hours' notice, it is well worth taking your money to France in French franc traveller's cheques. You will probably have to give your bank a week's notice to obtain them for you. French franc traveller's cheques can be changed at face value at any bank in France. Sterling traveller's cheques are subject to fluctuations in the pound at home. If the pound falls 10 per cent you may find that French banks will drop their exchange rate even lower until they see which way the pound will go. Losing 10 per cent of your holiday fund can be very alarming.

Check with your bank the right procedure to follow should the cheques be lost or stolen. Read carefully the instruction sheet given to you with the cheques. Ask for your money in larger rather than smaller denominations. Why carry a more bulky package than necessary?

If you are planning your holiday several months in advance it is well worth studying day to day movements in exchange rates. Picking the best day on which to buy your foreign currency can reduce the cost of your holiday by quite a useful margin, and you do not need to be an accountant to do it.

Before leaving home divide your cheques into three separate lots. A thief is unlikely to find all three. I usually carry a third of our cheques, my wife has the same while the remainder is hidden in the car or our baggage.

Never leave it to the last minute to change your next lot of traveller's cheques. Banking hours are different in France and different again from town to town and bank to bank. In some towns the banks do not open at all on a Monday. In some places you can find a bank that opens on a Saturday morning.

Whenever you present yourself at the counter of a French bank be sure to carry your passport, it is almost certain you will be asked to produce it.

Remember that at midday every day France turns into a pumpkin. Absolutely everything, except cafés and restaurants, are closed from 12 noon until 2pm and sometimes until 3 or even 3.30pm.

Cash Before leaving the UK make sure you have sufficient cash in French francs to last you through the first 48 hours. If you are crossing by Sealink you may find yourself on a French boat which will prefer payment at the shops and restaurants in francs. On every boat there is a *bureau de change* but you may not obtain the best exchange rate and you may have to queue. (There are no facilities for changing money on board Hovercraft.)

Also ask your bank to supply you with about 50 francs in coins. Many of the motorway service areas sell hot drinks only from vending machines. It is also useful to have change for motorway tolls. Some are now automatic coin-in-the-slot type.

Note When travelling always carry enough money in cash to cover all your immediate costs. Many French hoteliers will not accept traveller's cheques or credit cards. This applies even to some of the larger international hotel groups.

Credit Cards Barclaycard is the most useful credit card to carry in France. You may use it at any shop or garage displaying the Visa-Carte Bleue sign. About 50 per cent of garages in France will accept payment by Carte Bleue.

Outside of Paris and a handful of major cities you are unlikely to see an Access logo in France. But do not despair, the Access

people have arranged a tie-up with Eurocard. Look for their sign: the big E with a flaming tongue — your Access Card will be very welcome there.

Diners Club is accepted by the more expensive restaurants and hotels, also by quality shops in some of the larger cities.

American Express is accepted by some of the more expensive restaurants but be careful . . . when you ask if they accept American Express make sure they know you are proffering a credit card and not American Express traveller's cheques.

Cashing Cheques Most banks in France will encash a British personal cheque for up to 50 pounds if accompanied by a Eurocheque card. Ask your bank to supply you with the appropriate card. Barclaycard or Access Card are not suitable for this purpose in France. A special Eurocheque encashment card is now obligatory as UK cheque cards are no longer valid for continental use. (Some European banks are now insisting that foreign cheques will only be accepted if written on special Eurocheques.)

Warning Try to avoid carrying large sums in cash. Keeping your money safe while on holiday is a serious matter. Remember when travelling in a foreign country as a tourist, every petty crook that crosses your path has spotted you. He also knows you are carrying more money than the average man in the street. He just cannot wait for you to go to the beach and take your clothes off. Do not make it easy for him (or her).

Insurance There are various types of insurance cover available to you when you are going abroad. Consult your local broker or ask the AA or RAC. Most of the ferry firms also offer attractive terms. It is wise, if only for peace of mind and a more relaxed holiday, to be well insured.

Let us look briefly at the risks against which it would be sensible to take out insurance cover. In the end it must be your decision.

HEALTH: as members of the EEC, British visitors who are entitled to full UK benefits can obtain medical advice and treatment in France on the same basis as French nationals. To benefit from this agreement you must obtain Form E 111 before you go. (Your local Social Security office will tell you how to apply.) This covers about 80 per cent of specified medical costs incurred but you still have to pay the balance, so it is worth taking out personal medical insurance as well.

CAR INSURANCE: although the Green Card insurance document is no longer compulsory when visiting other EEC countries, it is very short-sighted not to ask your insurers to issue you with one before your leave. Whatever motor cover you

have at home will be reduced to third party only when you travel abroad without a Green Card.

ACCIDENT OR BREAKDOWN: the AA, RAC and the ferry companies all offer advantageous terms for motor recovery and get-you-home service in the event of accident or serious breakdown. Your local insurance broker can also advise.

LOSS AND THEFT: ask your broker about an all risk policy to protect against loss or theft.

Driving in France

The standard of driving in France is high and, we believe, better than in the UK. This is certainly true on motorways where you rarely see vehicles travelling in the fast lane. A French driver will never change lanes on a motorway without using his flashing indicator which he often leaves switched on until he pulls back in again. In France the fast lane really is for overtaking and that applies to visitors as well.

The reputation of British motorists in France is not good and the accident rate is high. Nevertheless, each year hundreds of thousands of us enjoy a trouble-free run to and from our destinations.

Accidents to British holiday-makers seem to happen mostly in the first 100 miles out from Calais, often due to hesitation, or in the last 200 miles on the way back, due to fatigue — accidents are often caused by a tired driver trying to make unnecessary haste to catch a ferry before it sails. Please remember that there is another ferry an hour or so later and if you have an open return ticket (see pp. 13-14) you can board the first ferry with space available when you arrive at the Channel port.

It is a very simple matter to adapt to driving on the right-hand side of the road. It helps to think of it as lane discipline.

Great care is necessary when overtaking. Following close behind another vehicle must be avoided. When driving from the nearside seat your vision becomes dangerously restricted if you are following another vehicle too closely.

My wife and I have proved a very simple code whereby we help each other with overtaking. The view from the passenger seat of a right-hand drive car is far better than the driver's view. If I am driving and pull out slightly to obtain a view past a heavy lorry, it is my wife who first sees the road ahead. She simply says Yes or No.

No means No, so I pull in again. Yes does not mean yes it is clear. It means: in her opinion, it is safe for me to pull out and view the road ahead and take a decision on whether or not it is safe to overtake. This avoids all those quite unhelpful remarks such as, 'I am not sure', 'I do not know' or 'What do you think?'.

It also gives the passenger a chance to contribute something helpful without taking decisions which must be the responsibility of the driver alone.

If possible share the driving with another person. If you can adapt to driving on the other side of the road so can your wife. Who knows she may turn out to be better than you.

Never, on these long-distance drives, stay behind the wheel for more than two hours at a time. If you do you are placing yourself, car, family and other road users in danger. Take frequent breaks and if possible walk some distance each time you stop.

In France drivers on main roads do not necessarily have priority over those emerging from roads on the right. This applies particularly in towns. So if a Frenchman shoots out of a side road right in front of you he may well have right of way. It is probably you who missed the road sign *Priorité à droite* (you must give way to traffic emerging from your right). Be careful. Frenchmen are very fragile, more so when riding bicycles and mopeds. If you do not see a sign which reads *Passage Protégé* (you have right of way over traffic emerging from your right), then watch that side road carefully.

France is in the process of changing the system of priority at roundabouts. Where you see a roundabout sign similar to the sign used in the UK (a circle formed by three arrows), then traffic on the roundabout has right of way.

French Garages

Over the years we have learned to have the highest respect for French garages and for the work of French garage mechanics. Of course, there must be exceptions to the rule but in general terms they are excellent.

It seems that a motorist in distress is given priority over regular customers. On numerous occasions we have been amazed to find a roadside garage prepared to drop what they were doing in order to get us under way again. It is a real bonus to encounter such service when you are in trouble.

Costs of repairs and spares seem to be very similar to UK prices. If, however, your vehicle has never been marketed in France, and this applies to quite a lot of Japanese cars, you will find that spares need to be shipped out from the UK.

Petrol The relative cost of a gallon of petrol in France and Britain has fluctuated greatly over recent years. Variations in the exchange rate make a considerable difference to the price.

When buying petrol in France we either ask for 50 or 100F (*cinquante francs* or *cent francs*, about £5 or £10 worth), or we say: *Le plein s'il vous plaît* (fill it right up). About half the garages in France accept payment by Barclaycard — you can use it where you see the sign Visa-Carte Bleue.

Oil In France engine oil is more expensive than in Britain. The smallest measure on sale is a 2-litre can (about half a gallon).

Remember to check your oil more frequently than you would at home. You will probably cover the equivalent of an average month's motoring in the first two or three days. Temperatures are much higher.

Roads

The roads in France fall into three main categories: A, N and D. Those prefixed A are *autoroutes* (motorways), those prefixed N (or RN) are *routes nationales*, main roads roughly equivalent to A roads in the UK. These trunk roads are all maintained by the national government. Minor or secondary roads, often prefixed D, are the responsibility of the local authority *(Département)*.

The network of N roads through France is excellent. Many drivers accept paying high tolls to use the autoroutes, leaving the N roads remarkably fast flowing and free from congestion.

Rules of the Road

Seat Belts Drivers and front seat passengers are required under French law to wear seat belts at all times. If you are stopped in a routine check and your belt is not fastened you face an on-the-spot fine.

It is illegal to carry a child under 11 years in the front seat of a motor vehicle.

Sometimes the fines handed out to drivers of foreign cars are quite nominal; the Gendarmerie tend to be generous towards visitors. But — they can hold you at the spot for up to two hours before they decide to be generous or otherwise.

Speed Limits

Motorways	130kph	or	81mph
Dual carriageways	110kph	or	69mph
Other roads	90kph	or	56mph
In towns	60kph	or	37mph
	or 45kph	or	28mph

The French police have instructions to enforce these speed limits rigidly and radar traps are much more common than in Britain. In Britain it is also hoped that the police will grant a 10 per cent tolerance on speed limits. Not so in France: 90kph means 90kph and at 91kph you could receive a very nasty fine to be paid on the spot.

Overtaking in towns, or in any place where the limit is 60kph or less, is strictly forbidden.

Police France has three distinctly separate police forces:

Agent Police are based in every town or village and are responsible to the town council for local matters.

Gendarmerie Nationale have full responsibility for all highway matters and crime detection.

C.R.S. is really the riot squad, but they are called in if the Gendarmerie are unable to cope with an unusual situation. They attend major football matches and spend most of the summer keeping an eye on the hordes of visitors on the Côte d'Azur.

Police Patrols Police road patrols fall mainly into two categories. Both are run by the Gendarmerie Nationale.

The first group patrol in dark blue vans. They operate the radar traps and police busy junctions. The second group are the elite of the French police and they use motorcycles. It is worth remembering that these men *never* go on patrol alone. If you see a policeman on a motorcycle, there is another one not far away; he may be tucked in behind you.

Road Signs Most road signs are now international but below we record some that are found only in France:

PÉAGE (toll). Warning that you are entering a section of road where you will be required to pay tolls. Advance signs, eg: *section à péage 1000m*, indicate the distance remaining in which you can avoid the toll road if you wish.

PASSAGE PROTÉGÉ You have right of way over traffic emerging from your right.

PRIORITÉ À DROITE Traffic emerging from your right has right of way — you must give way to traffic from your right.

TOUTES DIRECTIONS sometimes AUTRES DIRECTIONS It means all directions or all other routes. There is no equivalent in common use in Britain. On a ring road or a route through a town it avoids the repetition on signs of a whole host of names. Keep following the *Toutes Directions* signs until the name of the place you are looking for appears on a separate sign.

CENTRE VILLE Towards town centre.

RAPPEL Reminder. (Usually displayed above a repeat of the sign about which it is reminding you — often the speed limit.)

ACCOTEMENTS NON STABILISÉS Road verges are soft ground.

CHAUSSÉE DÉFORMÉE Uneven road surface.

POIDS LOURDS Heavy lorries.

AIRE DE REPOS Rest area.

PAR BROUILLARD When foggy.

DÉVIATION Diversion.

SANS ISSUE No through road.

Road Numbers During the latter years of the de Gaulle regime a decree was issued whereby the numbering of French roads was to be reviewed and updated. In some parts of France the renumbering had been started before the subsequent government lost interest in the project. Sadly, that does not mean that it is now a case of: as you were. Some local authorities are still slowly going through the process of renumbering.

If you find a road that suddenly changes its number between two towns, or if the road you are following does not tally with the road number on the map, do not be unduly alarmed. It does not necessarily mean that you are lost but that you have fallen victim to the renumbering process.

Such roads usually have a 3, 6 or 9 either added to the front of the number or substituted for the first of the three numbers (thus the N33 may now be the D333).

If you feel fairly confident that you are on the right road, continue, and if the next place you come to is the one you expected then you have just come through one of the renumbered areas.

Kilometres to Miles

To convert kilometres to miles divide by 8 and multiply by 5 (8km is approximately 5 miles).

8km	=	5 miles
10km	=	6 miles
40km	=	25 miles
80km	=	50 miles
100km	=	62 miles

On modern cars the speedometer is calibrated in both miles and kilometres. At a glance you can see that 80kph is equivalent to 50mph.

So do not forget that this handy speed converter can also be used to convert distances. For example, if you see a sign that says Paris 80km — a glance at your speedo will show the distance to be 50 miles.

A coarse but handy rule of thumb for the

quick conversion of kilometres to miles is to half the number and add a tenth, eg 38km: 19 + 3.8 = 22.8mi (exact figure is 23.6mi).

Litres to Gallons
    5 litres   =   1.1 gallons
 20 litres   =   4.4 gallons
 50 litres   =   11.1 gallons
    It may help to remember the jingle: a litre of water's a pint and three-quarters.

Motorway Tolls
The latest table of French motorway tolls can be obtained from the French Government Tourist Office, 178 Piccadilly, London W1.

Lorries
All heavy lorries, other than those carrying perishable goods, are banned from French roads on Sundays. This means that main highways are far less congested, sadly it also means that all Relais Routier restaurants are closed.

Traffic lights
Sometimes at complicated junctions in large cities it is difficult to be certain which traffic light you should obey. The simple rule is that you stop only for a red light on your right.

An orange flashing light means you may proceed with caution. At certain times of the day some traffic lights are set to flash on orange: the same rule applies.

En Route

(Garages, petrol and oil on p. 22.)

Food and Drink

Water One of the standard first questions from new arrivals in France is: Can we drink the tap water? The short answer is usually yes, unless the tap is marked *eau non potable* (water not drinkable). Most Frenchmen get quite upset if it is suggested that their tap water is not fit for drinking. Despite this they rarely drink it themselves. Most prefer their favourite brand of spa water which they buy from the supermarket for about 2.00F per litre. For peace of mind you may also wish to buy bottled water to put in the children's drinks or, to make your holiday that little bit different, to make ice and to add to wine or pastis. But please do not go to the ridiculous length of using bottled water to clean your teeth.
Picnics French families love picnics. They flock to the countryside at weekends and holidays. There are many designated picnic areas even on the autoroutes. Facilities are very good and include seats and tables and sometimes a children's playground. The French will find a suitable spot and dine in some style, taking with them folding chairs, table complete with tablecloth, good food and, of course, wine.

If you have packed a picnic basket, as suggested on p. 18, you only have to pop into a baker's and buy a loaf of French bread to have yourself a picnic.
Roadside Snacks A rough notice nailed to a tree heralds the many roadside stalls selling snacks. The message is usually *Frites* (chips) but sausages and other savoury items are also frequently available. Sometimes you will spot a stall labelled *Boissons* or *Buvette* where softs drinks are sold, and there are lots of roadside fruit stands as you travel further south.
Motorway Service Areas Those towing touring caravans might well consider taking meals or even passing the night at a motorway service area. Parking is free and there are usually very good toilet facilities. There is also invariably enough space to allow you to park away from the immediate noise of passing traffic.

Restaurants and snack bars at service areas on the motorways vary enormously from very good to disgusting. They have only one common factor: they are very expensive.

In addition to full service areas French motorways also offer rest areas known as *Aires*. These do not have restaurants or filling stations but do offer toilet facilities. They are usually to be found in attractive wooded areas and are much more pleasant than service areas.

Les Relais Routiers In France the needs of the hungry motorist are catered for better than anywhere else in the world. The towns, villages and roadsides are a never-ending gourmet's paradise. Those on a restricted budget will welcome the Relais Routier restaurants (see p. 33).

Hotels

Do you have a room? *Avez-vous une chambre s'il vous plaît?*

The centre of many French towns is dominated by an impressive building styled *Hôtel de Ville* – this is not a hotel, it is the Town Hall.

Hotels in France are much cheaper than hotels in the UK and there are more of them. So if you plan an overnight stop at a hotel en route there are substantial savings to be made by crossing to France before you retire for the night.

Most small towns in France have several small hotels and it is usually quite easy to find accommodation all the year round. But be warned:

It becomes much more difficult to find hotel accommodation after 6 pm. The earlier in the day you enquire the easier your task.

Hotels in the Channel ports become very busy in July and August. It is worth driving a few miles inland to one of the smaller towns such as Ardres, St Omer or Montreuil.

When you find a hotel with a vacancy ask to see the room. (If you have no French, point to your eye then up the stairs and smile.) When you enter the room the price you will pay is clearly shown on the inside of the door. A room in a small hotel, quite good enough for one night, can still be found from 80F (about £8) for two people.

If, outside of Paris, you find yourself paying over 150F for two people you are in a very good hotel indeed.

The price of hotel accommodation in France is usually based on the total cost of room irrespective of the number of occupants. Quite often a family room for two adults and two children can be obtained for the all-in price of about £10. It seems a better deal than unpacking all the camping gear for one night en route.

At night many small hotels close and lock their doors at 10.30 or 11 pm. If you wish to leave early the next morning it is a good idea to settle your bill before you go to bed and to ascertain from which door you should depart next morning.

The pillows on most beds in French hotels are hard, sausage-shaped bolsters. Often an inspection of the room will reveal softer pillows hidden in a wardrobe. If not do ask for a pillow: *un oreiller* (pronounced or-eye-yeh).

Some useful words and terms:

Pension	Full board
Demi-pension	Half board
Une Chambre	A bedroom
Salle de Bain	Bathroom
Douche	Shower
Cabinet de Toilette	Washbasin and bidet
W.C.	Toilet
Petit déjeuner	Breakfast
Ascenseur	Lift
Escalier	Stairs

Signs: Shops & Services

The following is a list of shop, service and business signs you are likely to come across as you travel through France.

À EMPORTER Take-away
AGENCE or AGENT IMMOBILIER Estate agent
ATELIER Workshop
AVOCAT Solicitor

BANQUE Bank

BOISSONS Soft drinks
BOUCHERIE Butcher
BOULANGERIE Bakery
BOUTIQUE Women's clothes usually
BRASSERIE Bar (usually serving light meals)
BRICOLAGE Do-it-yourself materials

BROCANTE Secondhand goods
BUVETTE Soft drinks and snacks stall

CAFÉ Bar
CAISSE Cash desk
CENTRE COMMERCIAL Shopping centre
CHARCUTERIE Pork butcher
CHEVALINE Horse butcher

DAMES Ladies

ENTRÉE Entrance
ENTRÉE LIBRE Open to the public
ÉPICERIE Grocery shop

FERMÉ LE DIMANCHE Closed Sunday
FERMÉ LE LUNDI Closed Monday
FERMÉ LES FÊTES DE L'ANNÉE Closed on
  public holidays
FERMETURE ANNUELLE Annual holidays
FERMETURE HEBDOMADAIRE Weekly closing
  day

GARE Railway station
GENDARMERIE Police station (or barracks)

HOMMES Gentlemen
HÔPITAL Hospital
HORLOGERIE Clock repairs
HÔTEL Hotel
HÔTEL DE VILLE Town hall
HÔTEL-DIEU Hospital
HYPERMARCHÉ Hypermarket

LAVERIE Laundry
LÉGUMES ET FRUITS Greengrocery
LIBRAIRIE Bookshop
LOCATION For hire

MAGASIN Shop
MAGASIN DE JOUETS Toy shop
MAIRIE Town hall
MAISON DE LA PRESSE Stationers
MÉDECIN Doctor
MESSIEURS Gentlemen

NÉGOCIANT EN VINS Wine merchant
NOTAIRE Notary

OCCASION Secondhand

PÂTISSERIE Cake shop
PHARMACIE Chemist's shop
PLOMBIER Plumber
POLICE Police
PRESSING Dry cleaner
PTT Post office

QUINCAILLERIE Ironmonger

RESTAURANT Restaurant

SELF Self service
SERVICE LIBRE Self service
SOLDES Sale goods
SORTIE Exit
STATION SERVICE Petrol filling station
SUPERMARCHÉ Supermarket
SYNDICAT D'INITIATIVE Tourist information
  office

TABAC Tobacconist
TOILETTES Toilets
TRAITEUR Cooked and prepared foodstuffs

Z.I. (ZONE INDUSTRIELLE) Factory estate

Telephones

Using the Telephone

Many people like to make at least one call
home during their holiday, if only to make
sure that the cat has not run off with the
lodger. A French telephone may be puzzling
at first encounter, but it is a very good
system and easy to use.
Coin Operated Call Boxes The
equipment accepts the following coins: 20
centimes, 50 centimes, 1F and 5F. If,
however, you are making an international
call the centime coins serve no purpose. It is
a good idea to obtain a supply of one-franc
coins before you make your call.
   In order to operate the system lift the
receiver and then insert a supply of coins.
Through a glass window in the front of the
paybox you can see the unused coins you
have inserted.

As your call progresses the coins will disappear from sight one by one. You may add more coins as you wish. Any coins unused when you replace the receiver on the rest will be returned to you via a small tray in the base.

It is a good idea to start your call with two or three one-franc coins in the slot. It is unwise to feed the machine too many five-franc pieces for if you do encounter a faulty call box it may retain your coins.

To Dial First lift the receiver from the rest and insert coins. You should then hear a high-pitched continuous dialling tone.

When dialling on a French phone you will frequently hear a musical tone. There is no equivalent of this in Britain. It is a searching tone and indicates that the automatic selecting equipment in the exchange is searching for the number you have dialled. You should wait, it will be followed either by a ringing tone or the engaged signal.

Press button dials and digital money counters are now being introduced but otherwise the system is unchanged.

Local Calls For calls within the same *département* (county), simply dial the six-figure number.

Long Distance For calls to another *département* in France, dial 16, pause and listen for a change to a deeper tone. Then dial the two-figure area code for the *département* followed by the six-figure number.

Phoning the UK Dial 19 which will connect you to international — when you are connected to an international line you will hear a deeper dialling tone.

Then dial 44, the international code for the UK.

Then dial the local STD code as you would at home but *miss off the first zero*.

Then dial the number you are calling.

International Calls Dial 19, wait for the second tone, then dial 33 for the international operator.

Phoning from a Post Office You can telephone from any post office (PTT) in France. Go to the counter under the sign *Téléphone* and ask for a *cabine* (kiosk). You will be given a token with the number of the kiosk allocated to you.

You can make as many calls as you wish; they will be metered at the counter. When you have finished, return your token to the counter clerk who will tell you how much you owe for the call(s).

Phoning From Your Hotel Perhaps the easiest way to phone home is to write down the number you require and ask the hotel receptionist to place the call for you. However, you will certainly find this expensive. The call may carry a hotel service charge of up to 50 per cent.

Phoning From Cafés Most cafés (bars) in France permit their clients use of the telephone, although some restrict this service to local calls. The calls are metered or timed and charged at whatever rate the Patron (landlord) wishes. This is usually a very expensive way of making a phone call.

Phoning From PTT Caravans There are not enough coin operated call boxes on the Côte d'Azur to meet the demands of the summer holiday season. So from June to September the PTT (post office) set up telephone caravans at busy centres along the coast. They are bright blue and usually well signposted. Each has six to twelve phones.

You simply enter and receive a token from the receptionist. Make your calls and pay as you leave.

Transfer Charge Calls Dial 12 and when the operator comes on the line say that you want to telephone *PCV* (pronounced pay-say-vay). You will be expected to give the number you require in French. So find out how to pronounce the number in French and rehearse your piece before you dial 12.

Shopping

When shopping in France remember that everything is weighed in kilos (1 kilo equals about 2.2 pounds).

Whenever possible do the bulk of your shopping in a large supermarket or hypermarket. It is worth driving a few miles to find one as the savings are well worthwhile.

At the hypermarket you can buy all items of food such as meat, fish, fruit and vegetables. Produce is always fresh due to the extremely fast turnover.

It is a good idea to try to live and shop as the French do, and it will certainly save money. A small packet of cornflakes (English breakfast, the French do not eat them) will cost well over a pound. The cost of butter, jam and a fresh loaf of bread every morning (French breakfast) will cost much less.

We recently received a visit from a couple who were about to set off for a holiday in France. What food should we take with us they wanted to know. Without hesitation we said, 'We can give you a long list of things to bring back'.

Tobacco and Spirits Contrary to popular belief you are entitled to buy your allowance of duty-free goods on the outward journey as well as on your way home.

In France cigarettes and tobacco can only be sold by a licensed tobacconist *(Tabac)*; even major supermarkets cannot sell them. The Tabac is easily recognized by the red cigar sign displayed outside the premises. (Wherever tobacco is sold you can also buy stamps.)

Proprietary brands of whisky and gin can be purchased in supermarkets throughout France for about the same prices as at home, sometimes less. French brands of cigarettes are about half the price of a packet of cigarettes in the UK, British brands are not so cheap but still cost less than they do in the UK.

Post Cards and Stamps Wherever you buy picture post cards in France the shopkeeper will also supply you with postage stamps *(timbres)*. However, this is done only as a service and the shopkeeper supplies you with stamps at the same price at which he purchased them from the PTT *(Postes Télégraphes Téléphones,* post office). He will usually therefore refuse to sell you any extra stamps you may need to post letters. When buying post cards it is well worth shopping around as the price can vary considerably.

Tea *Thé* French teabags rarely suit British tastes. Take your own.

Coffee *Café* Instant coffee costs much the same as at home. Ground coffee and coffee beans are much cheaper and it is well worth taking some back with you.

Bread *Pain* Most of the bread sold in France is in the form of the stick loaf, the *baguette,* and very good it is too. To the surprise of many visitors bread is also available in a whole variety of shapes and sizes. Just as well, for it is all but impossible to make acceptable toast from a baguette.

In most towns and villages the family baker's shop *(Boulangerie)* will offer freshly baked bread at least twice a day. Although French bread is of high quality and of superb texture, it does not keep well. A baguette purchased one day is unlikely to stay fresh enough to be enjoyed at breakfast the following day. Many French housewives are out early to buy bread for breakfast, and often buy a fresh loaf before each subsequent meal during the day.

Although the Boulangerie will be open on Sunday morning in many parts of France, it will be closed all day on Monday. Your Monday bread can be purchased from the large supermarkets. Generally, supermarket bread is not of the same high standard as the village baker's but there are exceptions to the rule and we have noticed that supermarket bread seems to improve each year. Let us hope this does not mean the end of the village bakery industry which has so far survived so well.

Cakes *Gâteaux* French cakes are tempting, scrumptious and very expensive. Try to avoid the more elegant *Pâtisseries* (cake shops), you will obtain a much better buy at the hypermarket.

It is accepted practice in France to buy a cake from the baker's down the road, go into a café, order coffee or something to drink and eat your cake with it.

Meat *Viande* In most towns you will find there are several different types of butcher's shop:

Charcuterie
Pork and products made from pork
Chevaline
Horse meats
Boucherie
All other meats
Hypermarché

Most large supermarkets also have a butchery department which offers ready-cut joints. They are displayed in transparent wrapping and clearly labelled to show price and type.

Beef *Boeuf* French butchers cut their meat differently and this is most apparent in beef. Some of the cuts you see make you wonder if French cows look the same as ours. Butchers in most other countries cut across the grain leaving in the bones. French butchers cut along the muscles to produce boneless joints. The cattle in France, including the white Charolais, are usually grass fed which makes their meat lean. If you buy a joint for roasting, larding (threading strips of fat through the joint) is virtually a necessity.

Beef for stewing, etc., is often labelled *Bourguignon*, but check that you have a sharp knife before you buy.

Steak *Bifteck* Steaks are usually less tender than those we enjoy at home, but in restaurants this is offset by superb sauces. *Faux Filet* is a cut of pure lean beef.

Minced Steak *Steak-Haché* This is suitable for many dishes. If you order it in a restaurant it will look like a hamburger but it is 100 per cent beef and, of course, very tender. You will not see it on display at the butcher's as it is not minced until ordered.

Do not compare the price with minced meat at home as the French product is all steak.

Pork *Porc* Excellent whichever way you eat it. Pork is eaten by the French as frequently as we eat beef. Cooked, cured and presented in so many ways at the *Charcuterie*.

Veal *Veau* Very popular and plentiful in France.

Lamb *Agneau* Popular, though it can be a little expensive.

Rabbit *Lapin* Very good, especially when served in a creamy mustard sauce — *Lapin à la Moutarde.*

Poultry and Game A great variety of birds and cuts, very fresh, are available in most places. In some parts of France housewives still buy their chicken live and carry it home by the legs. (Rabbits are bought in the same way.)

Turkey escalope, *escalope de dindoneau,* is a very good buy. Quick and easy to cook, it is very tasty, especially with a packet sauce poured over.

Fish *Poisson* Fish stalls throughout France are magnificent, and most supermarkets have a large selection which is always fresh and displayed so artistically. Mussels *(moules),* prawns *(crevettes),* crab *(crabe)* and lobster *(homard)* are all good buys.

Fruit and Vegetables *Fruits et Légumes* Always very good all over France: fresh, inexpensive and in such wonderful variety. Supermarkets always have a section where you can select your own produce. Remember when you buy at a supermarket to have your goods weighed at the point of selection, before you go to the main checkout. If there is no price on the bag when you get there you will be asked to go back and have it weighed. The French sell far more vegetables by weight than we do — vegetables such as cauliflower *(chou-fleur)* and sometimes even lettuce *(salade).*

Cheese *Fromage* French cheese is available in a tremendous variety of shapes and textures and, when accompanied by French bread, what a superb meal it can be.

We now buy cheese from the pre-wrapped and priced section of the supermarket because several times in the past when we bought from the delicatessen counter it cost more than we had bargained for.

If you enjoy cheese France is the perfect place to experiment as there are over 500 different types from which to choose.

One cheese we must mention is Munster. We think it delicious *but* it is best to buy only the quantity you will consume that day as it has rather a pungent smell. We have a friend in France who keeps it in his letter box in the gatepost as his wife will not allow it in the house.

If at the deli counter you spot a lump of

cheese that looks like Cheddar — *faites attention* — it may be butter.

And do not forget, cheese is best served at room temperature, so remove from the refrigerator one hour before serving.

Butter *Beurre* Maybe a little more expensive than in the UK but not much, you can usually find a reasonably priced brand in the supermarket.

The French do not eat butter on their bread. You will seldom be served butter in a restaurant other than with cold meats.

Butter is used in a sandwich only when the filling is ham *(jambon)*. French butter is invariably unsalted — if you want to buy salted butter look for labels reading *demi-sel.*

Prepared Foods *Traiteur* One of the gastronomic wonders of France is the delicatessen counter. Even supermarkets boast a fantastic selection of cold meats, cheese, salads, vol au vents, pies, gâteaux, etc.

You could lay on a fabulous dinner party from the deli counter alone without doing any real preparation yourself.

General Foods Tinned vegetables are cheap and we think much better than the equivalent at home, especially the tins of tiny peas *(petits pois fins)*. Tinned pâté is a good buy. Tuna fish in tins is excellent and a very good basis for salads, especially *Niçoise.*

French packet soup — much tastier than the British version — served with French bread makes an excellent cheap meal. Packet sauces are also very good and easy to prepare:

Sauce au poivre vert Creamy pepper sauce
Sauce chasseur White wine with mushrooms
Sauce marchand de vin Red wine sauce.

Wine

In a wine-producing country like France you will pass many roadside signs relating to the sale of wine *(vin)*:

Dégustation Means you may taste the product. It does not say 'free of charge', but we have never been asked to pay for sampling the wine.

Co-operative A syndicate set up by local farmers to produce and sell the wine from their collective crops.

Gros ou détail Large or small quantities: *détail* means by the bottle, *gros* means in

bulk (you take your own container which will be filled from a nozzle — rather like buying a jerry can of petrol). By the way, the French call large plastic containers either jerry cans or *vracs.*

If you are buying only for consumption during your holiday there is no point in buying in bulk. We advise you to stick to the local supermarkets and sample all they have to offer. Perhaps one wine will prove so pleasant that you will stock up with a few extra bottles to take back home with you at the end of the holiday.

Wine to Take Home You may take into the UK four litres of wine (duty free), yes that is really eight litres per couple provided that you are not carrying other alcoholic liquids. It is really sad not to take advantage of this generous allowance from HM Customs and Excise. Your eight litre allowance, per couple, is about 12 bottles of 70cl. A very useful quantity of wine to bring home duty free.

Do remember that if you exceed the four litres per person, or carry additional alcohol, you must declare the difference to UK customs.

The duty you will be required to pay is currently over £1 per litre. The same rate of duty applies whatever the quality of wine you import, with the exception of sparkling wines such as Champagne. So better savings are made on the more expensive wines.

The customs procedure takes only five or ten minutes and is usually conducted in a spirit of complete harmony. If you take an extra bottle of Scotch into France, and declare it, the same procedure can take 24 hours and be very expensive.

Markets

Wherever you are staying in France it is well worth checking to see which day is market day. Most towns have at least one market *(marché)* each week. Sometimes the town square is taken over by the street traders; in smaller villages streets are sometimes closed to allow the market to take place. The stalls are set up early in the morning and by 8am the market is in full swing.

Fresh vegetables, beautifully presented, include a wonderful array of those familiar at home as well as exotic fruits and herbs rarely found in the UK. There are cheese stalls with an amazing range of produce and olive sellers offering a choice of green, black, pickled, large, small, salted, dried — and we thought they were just olives.

Many French housewives prepare fish for lunch on market days. Fish stalls are often owned by the fishermen themselves, and the produce comes straight from boat to stall.

It is not only foodstuffs that make the markets exciting; clothing is much cheaper than in the shops, yet most garments offered seem to be of acceptable quality.

The ironmongers' stalls are a sight to behold: no pre-packed packets of nails and screws for these merchants.

An hour or two spent at a market is an experience not to be missed. But do not leave it too late in the morning, for at midday the market will disappear as quickly as it came. By 2pm the street will have been cleaned and it will be difficult to believe there was ever a market there.

Cafés & Restaurants

Service

Do you remember service and the bygone custom of a shopkeeper telling you he appreciated your visits? Very rare now in the UK — but in France it is never forgotten. Almost every time you leave a shop or café you will do so to the echo of 'Au revoir Monsieur, Merci Monsieur, Madame'.

In restaurants and cafés the waiters will invariably spring to your aid the moment you take your seat; real service. It still exists in France.

Le Patron Although friendly and courteous the French tend to be very formal. To move a relationship onto a Christian name basis is a very big step indeed. When the Patron of a restaurant in La Croix-Valmer decided to drop M. Little and use Michael (Me-kell), we were quite delighted. It then took several more visits before he ventured to ask if he might address Madame by her Christian name. Of course we readily agreed but he seemed to have some problems pronouncing Rita. After spending several minutes wandering round the restaurant muttering to himself he returned to our table 'Pardon', he said 'but you did say Huit heures, isn't that Eight o'clock?' Rita has been known as eight o'clock ever since.

Warning Never address a waiter as *Garçon*. Many school books still translate waiter in this way but you must call him (or her) *Monsieur* (or *Madame*). To call a waiter *Garçon* is most unkind, only his boss will address him or refer to him in this way.

PSSTT! The word for draught beer is *pression* (pressy-on), and in cafés it is very much cheaper than bottled varieties.

Tipping

In all service industries in France tipping is an accepted practice and many waiters survive on their tips which form the greater part of their income. The usual custom is to add 10-15 per cent or more if you are pleased with the service when you pay your bill.

Many French bars and restaurants will add the 10-15 per cent to your bill before you receive it. The bill will usually be marked *service compris* (service included) in which case no further gratuity is expected.

Where service has not been included the bill will usually be marked *service non compris* or *prix net* (both mean that service is not included). You are then expected to add at least 10 per cent to the bill.

You have to be wary as sometimes such information is shown on the menu but not on the bill and, of course, you have parted with the menu long before you face the bill.

Occasionally you will receive a bill at a café which is marked neither *service compris* nor *service non compris*. In other words, for reasons of their own, the management are not telling you. In such cases give yourself the benefit of the doubt and do not tip.

Some bills will be submitted to you marked TTC or *Toutes Taxes Comprises* (all taxes — or TVA (VAT) — included). It does not necessarily mean that service is also included, but it is usually in there too. STC or *Service, Taxe Compris* means service and tax included.

Cafés

Cafés should not be confused with those

establishments in Britain which sadly bear the same name. The French café is the nearest equivalent to our pub or perhaps bar is a better description. Every café in France is required to display a tariff showing the prices of their wares. It is a mystery to most visitors why they are always charged more than the price displayed. If it is of any consolation the French also rarely pay tariff prices.

The landlord *(le Patron)* is only bound by his tariff prices if you stand at the bar to give your order, specify the exact measure shown on the tariff, and stand at the bar to down your drink. The slightest deviation from this procedure and he can charge you what he likes.

Most cafés in France charge prices higher than those shown on the tariff. This does not mean they are dishonest; they simply sell you a larger measure or a different brand and charge accordingly.

Nevertheless, one must be very cautious when using the seafront bars in the holiday resorts of the Côte d'Azur. You can be really ripped off. In fairness to the owners they have a ten week season in which to produce the revenue to pay their staff and their rent for a year. But do be careful and try to avoid drinking on terraces in front of cafés where there is waiter service, you will pay dearly for that service. Remember too that if you go to the bar and buy your round you are not entitled, at bar prices, to sit out on the terrace.

In a French café it is normal procedure not to pay for each round of drinks as you receive them. The waiter or Patron will open an account for you when you first order and present your bill when you depart. In most cases you will be given a slip of paper with the cost of each purchase clearly shown. It is always a good idea to check these slips as you receive them, do not wait until you have a pile of them before you discover you are being ripped off.

The most important factor in reducing your bar costs is what you actually order. You will reduce your costs considerably if you consume the same drinks as the French. To order a gin and tonic can be tantamount to committing financial suicide. No Frenchman ever drinks gin and tonic, and in the more remote parts of France you may have to explain what it is. While you are searching for the words to explain that it is a *gin avec schweppes*, the Patron is mentally calculating how much he thinks you can afford to pay for your strange drink.

A favourite faux pas made by English visitors is to order: *une bière, s'il vous plaît.* You might just as well carry a sign saying: I am a tourist, hit me. A Frenchman would say: *une demi s'il vous plaît,* and expect to receive a quarter litre of draught lager; that is right a quarter not a half as it suggests.

Why not drink wine, it is very cheap everywhere in France.

Restaurants

As we start to write this section the very thought of restaurants in France starts the digestive juices working.

To understand why there are so many French restaurants and why they are so good, it is first necessary to understand the eating habits of a Frenchman. Breakfast simply consists of very strong and very good coffee. The most a Frenchman will take with this is a croissant or a piece of bread.

At twelve o'clock France stops and the French eat. This will be at least two courses, usually three. The meal must be taken at table with wine and with adequate time for slow digestion. The French do not then eat again until their dinner in the evening. They rarely eat between meals and they never indulge in the sloppy habit of eating off their lap while sitting in an easy chair. Dinner will again be at least three courses with emphasis on quality rather than quantity.

The importance of meal times to the French is wonderfully reflected by the EDF (Electricity of France), who impose power cuts on their clients with a frequency unheard of in the UK. It is not uncommon to find that all power disappears about 9.30am. But of one thing you can be absolutely certain, power will be resumed a little before noon so that lunch can be prepared. It will then quite possibly be cut off again about 2pm until late afternoon.

When a Frenchman is travelling he will not vary from his normal habits, he cannot eat at home so he will eat in a restaurant.

The growth of heavy transport on the

roads since World War Two has resulted in a parallel growth in the number of restaurants to allow lorry drivers to dine as if they were at home. Their needs are served by a chain of individually owned restaurants called Les Relais Routiers. The striking blue and red signs of the Routier restaurants are found every few miles throughout France. They are without doubt the best value for money in the world. Although there is rarely a wide choice of dishes the quality is usually superb. One can expect a three-course menu from about 35F (about £3) and often half a litre of wine is included in the price.

There are so many Relais Routiers that they must obviously vary in quality and value for money. When journeying through France, perhaps on a route we have never previously used, we can still pick out the better Routier restaurants at a glance. Sometimes we will pass three or four Routiers before we spot the one we are seeking out. Suddenly there it is, surrounded by a pack of juggernauts which may actually be obscuring the restaurant. Trust the French lorry driver's judgement, he is never wrong.

Eating in an unknown town is a problem anywhere in the world. When on strange ground how do you decide which restaurant to patronize. Every restaurant in France has the menu displayed outside the premises. Half an hour before dinner spent strolling round town looking over the menus can really pay dividends. Do not forget to look in the back streets and alleys. Restaurants are often tucked away in the strangest places. Do not choose a restaurant which is nearly empty. Somewhere in town there will be one so full of locals that you may even have to share a table, but why not? When in Rome . . .

Eating à la carte in France can be quite expensive, but even the very best restaurants will offer a set menu at a fixed price. You may expect a choice of three starters, two or three main courses, sweet and cheese. Look for signs that say: Menu at 39F, Menu at 50F, etc.; over 70F is getting expensive.

At a restaurant in Saulieu we once complimented the Patron on his beef. He dashed off to fetch a photograph of a prize cow that had recently won the local contest

for Miss Charolais. He explained that he had bought the whole carcass and we were indeed honoured to have partaken of such meat.

Most restaurants in France lay the table with a paper tablecloth which is replaced at every sitting. This is usually spread over a linen cloth which falls to your lap. The paper cloth on top is yours — very often by the end of a meal the French clientele will have covered their cloth with drawings, figures and sketches. Ours is usually well covered with route maps and travel costs. Think of the waiters who threw away Picasso's doodles.

Many French towns offer no facilities for snacks, although a sandwich in French bread can be obtained at some cafés. Larger towns will perhaps have a brasserie or two where you can obtain snacks and sandwiches. The French are not a nation of snack eaters.

Most of the large hypermarkets have self-service restaurants where you can obtain a very good cheap meal. Not a gourmet's paradise but a chance to take all the kids out to eat and not hit the budget too hard.

If you have children who like big gooey ice creams, remember that many hypermarkets sell them at about half the price you would pay in cafés and ice cream parlours.

Wine in Restaurants There is not much point in shopping around for a cheap, value-for-money menu and then blowing everything you saved on an expensive bottle of wine. But first-time visitors to France often discover that their restaurant bill is higher than they expected and the most usual explanation is that they asked for *vin du pays* or *vin ordinaire*.

Most restaurants in France offer a low-priced red wine sold by the jug *(pichet)*, of which they are justifiably proud. The Patron will have selected his house wine *(cuvée du patron)* only after rejecting many contenders offered by the local wine merchants. Why is it then so difficult to persuade him to sell it to you?

At home the head waiter comes to your table to take your valued order, in France the same applies up until the moment you mention wine. Then your friendly head waiter should be regarded as a salesman working on commission only. If you ask for a *vin du pays* he will quite possibly serve you an expensive local wine.

If you really want to drink the Patron's low-priced pride and joy, you should order *cuvée du patron*. If he pretends not to understand then state clearly: *vin de la maison*, house wine. Remember that you are expecting to be brought a jug and not a bottle. If he brings out a bottle just say *pichet* (pee-shay) firmly.

Only red wines come by the jug. Drinking white wine in restaurants in some parts of France can be quite expensive. The French are really a nation of red wine drinkers. White and rosé are saved for special dishes, special occasions and sunshine days.

Typical Menu in a French Restaurant

Charcuterie
A selection of cold meats.

Crudités
A selection of salads served with oil: eg, tomatoes, cucumber, raw carrots, celeriac, red cabbage, etc.

Soupe de Poisson
Fish soup, a favourite starter in Provence. A tureen of soup is served with a dish of croutons, some grated cheese and a dish of Rouille (a very strong sauce). You spread two or three croutons with the sauce, place in the bottom of your bowl, then ladle the soup over and sprinkle the cheese on the top.

Côte de Porc
A pork chop, usually succulent and always well cooked.

Steak Grillé
Grilled steak. In most restaurants it is simply a thin steak.

Steak au Poivre
If a peppered steak (or fillet steak) is on the menu you will often be required to pay a supplement on top of the set price. The steak will be a much thicker cut. Do not forget to say how you would like your steak cooked, or it will be served to you very, very red: well done *(bien cuit)*, medium *(à point)*, rare *(bleu)*.

Moules Marinières
Mussels served in a creamy garlic sauce: a marvellous excuse for using lots of French bread and 'dunking' which is completely acceptable in France even in the better restaurants.

Plat du Jour
Dish of the day. Well worth while enquiring what is on offer. It is usually a fresh and original, sensibly priced main course which changes daily. In some restaurants available only at lunch, not at dinner.

Glace
Ice Cream
Tarte Maison
Home-made tart
Crème Caramel
Cream caramel

Fromage
Cheese, not always from a cheese board, depends on the restaurant. Very often a choice of Brie or Camembert or, if you are lucky, Roquefort. No biscuits or butter but more fresh bread if you wish.

NB If you are looking for the very best steak, and you are prepared to pay for it, ask for *steak pavé* (parvay).

Snack Foods from Brasseries and Cafés
Pan Bagnat: a large round roll (about 15cm/6in across) filled with all kinds of salad and tuna fish topped with a dressing. A meal on its own. Found only in the south of France. *Croque Monsieur:* a toasted sandwich with ham and cheese filling. *Croque Madame:* The same thing but with a fried egg on top. *Sandwich:* usually half a French loaf with a choice of fillings, generally: pâté, cheese (usually Brie or Camembert) or ham (this is the only type of sandwich with butter). *Coupe:* a mixture of ice cream and fruit in a large glass topped with Chantilly cream.

Tea *Thé* The first French word an Englishman abroad will learn is tea. Written *thé* it is pronounced tay.

Unless you specify that you require milk it will always be served black. Tea with milk is *thé au lait.*

Sun and Sand

The Climate

Coastal Regions From the oranges and lemons of the south to the vast wheat fields of the north, from the Alpes and the deep Gorges du Verdon in the south to the sugar beet plains in the north, France is a country of geographical and climatic contrasts. There are three distinct coastlines: the English Channel, the Atlantic and the Mediterranean, and all three also have quite different climates.

In the north, the Channel coast round Normandy is a daisychain of small fishing villages interspersed with an occasional busy port such as Le Havre. The climate here is much the same as in the southern part of England.

The Atlantic coast starts in the north west at the rocky Finistère peninsula, runs south to the point where the River Garonne joins the Dordogne, forming the Gironde estuary, and finishes in 240km/150 miles of fine sand all the way to the mouth of the Adour at Biarritz on the Spanish frontier. The climate is as warm as the latitude suggests, but it is also a region which experiences more rain than most parts of France; the Dordogne has recorded levels of rainfall on a par with Manchester.

The Mediterranean coast, from the Pyrénées to where the Camargue absorbs the Rhône estuary, consists of 192km/120mi of sandy beaches which, up until the 60s, lay undeveloped and largely inaccessible. Then comes the Carmargue itself, a strange flat area of marshland and shallow lakes. From Marseille eastwards to the Italian border the coastline becomes quite spectacular with rocky coves at the foot of mountains that rise out of the sea. The climate is one of the most agreeable in the world. Hot summers, mild winters and balanced rainfall make the Riviera coast a most attractive place to live. The lucky inhabitants can count on two or three light frosts each winter and fog about every ten years.

The Mistral Without warning, though keen gardeners seem to be able to forecast its coming, the Mistral may hit the south of France at any time. These incredibly strong winds, often reaching severe gale force, are quite frequent events in Provence. Sometimes two or three months elapse without the Mistral making its appearance but it can, particularly in winter, occur twice or even three times in a month.

The Mistral sometimes performs at full strength day and night without respite. Its wrath, however, is always short-lived, usually lasting 48 hours; 72 hours is almost unknown. Most locals will tell you the Mistral comes one day, plays havoc on the second and dies away to nothing on the third.

This strange phenomenon comes not from the sea but from the mountains of Switzerland far to the north. It builds up in strength as it huffs, puffs and then explodes down the Rhône Valley to batter and pummel unprepared visitors to Provence.

The Beach

As a general rule beach requisites, with the exception of swimwear, are best purchased in France, but never buy them at the shop on the beach. Sun tan oil, air beds and parasols can be purchased at hypermarkets for a fraction of the price demanded by beach sellers.

Most beaches in the south of France are non-tidal and have both private and public sections; the latter cost nothing and you use them exactly as you would the beach back home. The private beaches cost between £3 and £6 per day (per person) for the use of sunbed and parasol supplied by the establishment. The private beaches are laid out each day, on meticulously prepared stretches of sand, and usually have a café or restaurant as a focal point. Drinks and meals can be served to you as you lie in the sun.

Wherever you choose to be on the beach you can expect frequent visits from strolling beach traders. You will be offered goods ranging from ice cream and fruit to little English rock cakes from a biscuit tin carried by a naked English lady. Most of the beach traders are in fact English students working through their summer vacation.

In recent years the Côte d'Azur has been invaded each summer by beach traders from Senegal and the Ivory Coast (and Toulon). They expect you to haggle over the price of their goods — you can usually expect to pay about 60 per cent of the asking price. Be careful when buying articles which appear to be made of ebony or ivory, make sure they are not plastic. You can often spot the marks where the injection moulding points have been filed off.

At the better beaches, such as Neptune on the Pampelone beach near St Tropez, you can rent sailing craft and windsurfers. We have hired one of the latter and tried to emulate the antics of those who have mastered the art. We only managed to produce a variation on the sport which we call wind jumping. This consists of jumping aboard, struggling for balance then jumping back into the sea, then jumping aboard, etc., etc.

Children's Drinks In a hot climate to which they are not accustomed, children can consume frightening amounts of soft drinks. To buy such drinks at cafés, particularly beach cafés, can be a very expensive pastime. A small (¼-litre) Coca-Cola in a beach café can cost as much as £1; in a French supermarket you can buy a litre bottle for the equivalent of 30p.

Barbecues This marvellous style of open-air cooking seems ideal in a warmer climate. But if you are going to stay in a place for the first time do not rely on the fact that you will be able to use a barbecue. Many places, including most camp sites, do not allow barbecues because of the high fire risk.

If you know you are permitted a barbecue but do not possess one, then buy it in France. They are much cheaper there. We bought a cast-iron barbecue, in 1983, from a hypermarket for £11.50.

Where does that car come from?

The last two digits on a French car number plate tell you where the owner lives in France.

If he moves home to another *département* he must re-register his car.

Départements (counties) of France

01 Ain	51 Marne
02 Aisne	52 Haute-Marne
03 Allier	53 Mayenne
04 Alpes-de-Hte.-Provence	54 Meurthe-et-Moselle
05 Hautes-Alpes	55 Meuse
06 Alpes Maritimes	56 Morbihan
07 Ardèche	57 Moselle
08 Ardennes	58 Nièvre
09 Ariège	59 Nord
10 Aube	60 Oise
11 Aude	61 Orne
12 Aveyron	62 Pas-de-Calais
13 Bouches-du-Rhône	63 Puy-de-Dôme
14 Calvados	64 Pyrénées-Atlantiques
15 Cantal	65 Hautes-Pyrénées
16 Charente	66 Pyrénées-Orientales
17 Charente-Maritime	67 Bas-Rhin
18 Cher	68 Haut-Rhin
19 Corrèze	69 Rhône
20 *See 2A and 2B below*	70 Haute-Saône
21 Côte-d'Or	
22 Côtes-du-Nord	
23 Creuse	
24 Dordogne	
25 Doubs	
26 Drôme	
27 Eure	
28 Eure-et-Loir	
29 Finistère	
30 Gard	
31 Haute-Garonne	
32 Gers	
33 Gironde	
34 Hérault	
35 Ille-et-Vilaine	
36 Indre	
37 Indre-et-Loire	
38 Isère	
39 Jura	
40 Landes	
41 Loir-et-Cher	
42 Loire	
43 Haute-Loire	
44 Loire-Atlantique	
45 Loiret	
46 Lot	
47 Lot-et-Garonne	
48 Lozère	
49 Maine-et-Loire	
50 Manche	

71 Saône-et-Loire	85 Vendée
72 Sarthe	86 Vienne
73 Savoie	87 Haute-Vienne
74 Haute-Savoie	88 Vosges
75 Seine-Paris	89 Yonne
76 Seine-Maritime	90 Territoire-de-Belfort
77 Seine-et-Marne	91 Essonne-Paris
78 Yvelines-Paris	92 Hauts-de-Seine-Paris
79 Deux-Sèvres	93 Seine-St Denis-Paris
80 Somme	94 Val-de-Marne-Paris
81 Tarn	95 Val-d'Oise-Paris
82 Tarn-et-Garonne	
83 Var	2A Corse-du-Sud Corsica
84 Vaucluse	2B Haute-Corse Corsica

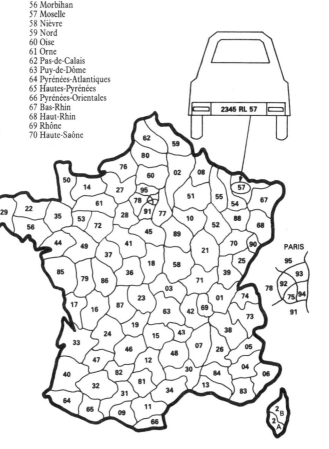

The Seven Wonders of France

We thought it would be fun to list our idea
of the seven wonders of France, so we put
together the following. We would be very
interested to learn what you would include
on your list of man-made and natural
wonders of France.
   The Eiffel Tower
   Gorges du Verdon
   Le Mont-St-Michel
   Le Pont St Nazaire
   Le Palais de Versailles
   Mont Blanc
   Roman Theatre at Arles

   We decided not to include the Cafe de
Paris, St Tropez, or the Euro rest at la
Palme, but both are well worth a visit.

Afterword

   Changes are inevitable. Towns with no
bypass are forever trying to find an
improved route for through traffic. Some
towns provide different routes for north and
south bound traffic, others have a different
route for heavy vehicles *(poids lourds)* which
may or may not include caravans. And every
autumn sees the usual crop of new bypasses.
   Nevertheless, we would be pleased to hear
how you found our routes. Did we save you
any frustration, or did we cause you to get
lost in that damn town that holds its market
on the bypass?

Write to us at:
Collins Travel Guides,
P.O. Box, Glasgow G4 0NB.

Route One
Calais – Paris N1
267km/166mi

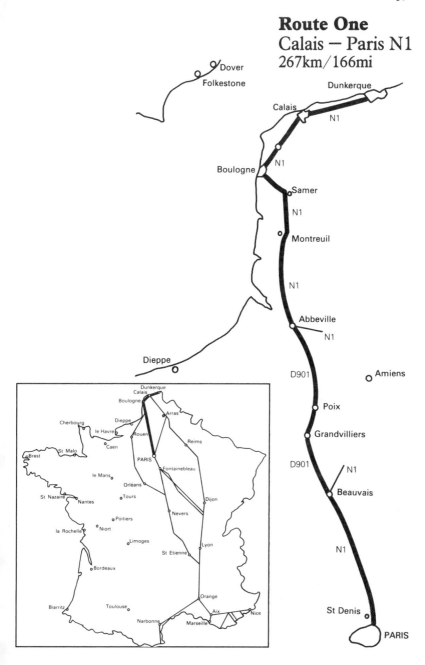

Route One   Calais — Paris N1

CALAIS

The massive investment in ferry passenger
terminal facilities which have been made by the
town of Calais clearly indicates the value placed by
the town council on its cross-Channel ferry business. So, too, do the excellent roads from the port
which will shortly link it into the French motorway
system.

Immediately you drive ashore you are in no
doubt that France begins at Calais. A bustling town
where you can buy and enjoy everything that is
French.

When you leave the port, continue 457m/
500yds to the roundabout and into Calais through
the industrial area. Turn right and then left (over
canal). Follow carefully signs N1 or RN1
BOULOGNE. (These refer to Route Nationale One.
The N and RN roads are roughly equivalent to A
roads in the UK.)

MARQUISE

Follow the N1 through this straggly little town,
famous for its marble quarries.

BOULOGNE

As you enter Boulogne and drive past the old
walled city which dominates the town, you may
well become quickly aware of the signs which say
'Pssst! Go Boulogne next time — save petrol and
money'. They really do have a point. It is a great
pity that Boulogne does not back up its advantage
in miles by matching the superb facilities at Calais.

If you choose to land at Boulogne, you will have
saved some 34km/21mi of uninteresting road
from Calais.

Leaving Boulogne on the outskirts of the town at
Pont-de-Brique, there is a junction where it is easy
to take the wrong fork. Watch carefully for the sign
into the left fork for PARIS: it will save you an unnecessary detour down the road towards Le Touquet.

Follow the N1, now signposted for ABBEVILLE,
SAMER and MONTREUIL-SUR-MER (which is not on
the sea!)

MONTREUIL
General Haig's headquarters in 1916.

The N1 now bypasses the old town of Montreuil and sweeps through avenues of trees, typical of northern France, towards ABBEVILLE.

ABBEVILLE
The town centre was completely destroyed in World War Two.

Negotiating the town is not difficult although there is no true bypass. The inner ring road bypasses the town centre. It is simply a case of watching for the overhead signs — just slot yourself beneath the ones for BEAUVAIS and PARIS. We strongly recommend that you do not take the N1 diversion from Abbeville to Beauvais through Amiens. It seems an unnecessary sidetrack.

Selecting the signs for BEAUVAIS and PARIS, you follow the D901 through hilly country, dropping into the sleepy town of Poix. Then you climb again to Grandvilliers and onto a plateau from which Beauvais can be seen in the distance.

BEAUVAIS
The 13th-century cathedral of St Pierre is the tallest in France. In 1940, it survived an air raid that wiped out every building surrounding it.

Beauvais is circumnavigated on an inner ring road but it is quite easy to negotiate by following the signs which read PARIS.

After the town, the N1 improves and is fast-flowing through wooded country to the outskirts of Paris at St Denis.

ST DENIS
As you arrive in the suburbs, be careful not to be drawn into the town centre of St Denis (avoid St Denis − Centre Ville). Follow the signs for PARIS. You will then pick up the blue motorway signs that lead down a short stretch of free motorway signed PARIS towards the Périphérique. (Paris ring road.) See Route Two page 49.

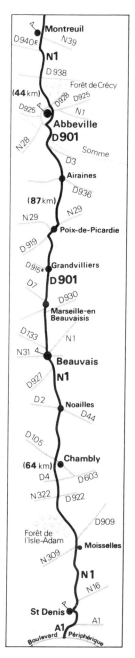

Route Two
Paris Ring Road
Périphérique

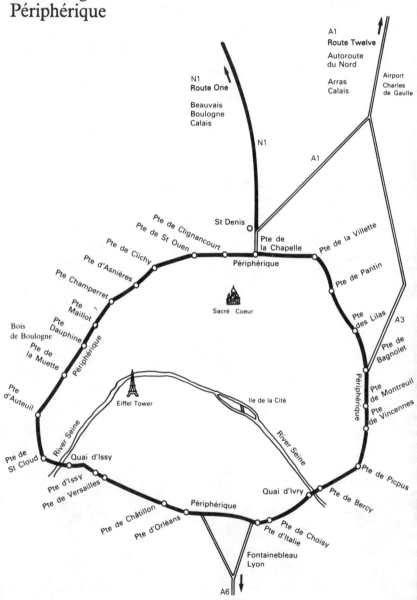

N1
Route One

Beauvais
Boulogne
Calais

N1

A1
Route Twelve

Autoroute
du Nord

Arras
Calais

Airport
Charles
de Gaulle

A1

St Denis

Pte de Clignancourt

Pte de St Ouen

Pte de Clichy

Pte d'Asnières

Pte Champerret

Pte Maillot

Pte Dauphine

Bois de Boulogne

Pte de la Muette

Périphérique

Pte de la Chapelle

Périphérique

Pte de la Villette

Pte de Pantin

Sacré Coeur

Pte des Lilas

A3

Pte de Bagnolet

Périphérique

Pte de Montreuil

Pte de Vincennes

Pte d'Auteuil

Eiffel Tower

River Seine

Ile de la Cité

River Seine

Pte de St Cloud

Quai d'Issy

Pte d'Issy

Pte de Versailles

Pte de Picpus

Pte de Châtillon

Périphérique

Pte d'Orléans

Quai d'Ivry

Pte de Bercy

Pte de Choisy

Pte d'Italie

Fontainebleau
Lyon

A6

Route Two

The Paris Ring Road
(Boulevard Périphérique)

When driving from the Channel ports to the south of France, it is not necessary to venture anywhere near Paris. See Route Four via Rouen and Orléans passing Paris to the west and Route Three via Reims, Dijon and Chalon passing Paris to the east. However, all the faster routes to the Mediterranean demand that you head for Paris and pass around the Périphérique ring road. There are no toll charges on the sections of motorway entering and leaving Paris or for use of the Périphérique.

The first-time visitor to France will naturally be apprehensive about driving through Paris but with very little preparation it can prove to be easy. However, it is sensible to avoid rush hour periods. Traffic on the Périphérique often grinds to a halt between 7.30am and 9.30am and 5pm and 6.30pm (8pm on Friday evenings). It is also wise to avoid lunch hour traffic from midday to 12.30pm and from 1.30pm to 2pm. Why not rest five minutes in a convenient café or lay-by and study Route Two, before you go further.

Boulevard Périphérique is rather like a ship's steering wheel: it is a complete circle with the centre of Paris at the hub. The routes converging on the city from every direction form the spokes of the wheel. Where each incoming route joins the Périphérique, there is a *Porte*. (The ancient gates to the city.) Today each Porte is a well-signposted, modern road junction rather like British motorway junctions.

The Périphérique is of motorway standard with three or four lanes in each direction. Built mostly on stilts above existing roads and buildings, it offers stupendous views over Paris to Sacré-Coeur (the Wedding Cake Church) and the Eiffel Tower. At some points, the Périphérique dives into well-lighted short tunnels to pass natural and man-made hazards. Traffic is usually very heavy but free-flowing apart from rush hours and public holidays.

Because the Périphérique is a complete circle, it does not matter whether you go round clockwise or anti-clockwise. We prefer to go Paris Est (east side of Paris) when going south, and we prefer Paris Ouest (west side of Paris) when going north. Travel in whichever direction you find easier — it does not matter at all.

As you approach the Périphérique you will see overhead signs indicating which lane you should take for PARIS EST and PARIS OUEST. Why not just stay in the lane in which you find yourself? Follow either the EST or the OUEST signs until you emerge through the junction onto the Périphérique.

Remember you must pass under each overhead sign. Be prepared for the swing to the right or left onto the Périphérique.

If entering the Périphérique by the A13 from Le Havre or Dieppe, follow the signs for PARIS SUD (south Paris). You are now on the Périphérique and circling Paris.

Each exit from the Périphérique is marked with the name of the ancient exit gate: Porte de la Chappelle, Porte de la Villette, Porte de Pantin and so on. The exit onto the main route to the south lies between Porte d'Italie and Porte d'Orléans (the gate for Italy and the gate for Orléans).

As you pass by each Porte, the name of the next one is shown on an overhead sign above the carriageway. If you are travelling fast in the outside (left-hand) lane, the overhead sign is a warning to work your way over to the near-side (right-hand) lane in advance of your exit.

You must be sure not to miss the sign for LYON (A6) — just think Lyon, Lyon, Lyon.

When you spot the exit point, the slip road will whip you away from the Périphérique into a brightly-lit tunnel. Immediately after entering the tunnel, you encounter a sharp bend and then, only seconds later, you emerge onto the motorway to the south — Autoroute du Soleil (A6).

You have done it — now that was not too bad was it?

If you are travelling homeward, towards the north, please note the following warning: on the west side of Paris (Paris Ouest) between Porte de St Cloud and Porte Maillot there is a sign to the largest park in Paris which is called the Bois de Boulogne.

The road sign just reads Boulogne. Many British travellers, over-anxious to be clear of Paris take this road thinking it is to the town of Boulogne and find themselves lost in the park. Ignore the sign and pass it by.

Watch for the sign to ROUEN if you are heading for Dieppe or Le Havre or to LILLE if you are heading for Calais or Boulogne.

Leaving Paris to the south by the A6 motorway, there is no toll for some 50km/30mi to a point near Fontainebleau.

Those going to south-west France will need to look out for the fork in the motorway signed ORLÉANS. This leads onto the A10 motorway (turn to Route Sixteen, page 108).

For those going on south there are three choices of route. You can continue all the way by motorway paying tolls (Route Twelve, page 90).

The other two routes take you to Lyon by the N6 and the Rhône Valley by the N7. The N7 is more picturesque but should be avoided in the early morning and between November and April due to mist.

For both routes, leave the motorway on the slip road signed FONTAINEBLEAU – NEVERS PAR RN. (It is not necessary to enter the town of Fontainebleau, though it is well worth a visit.)

This road continues for several miles, signed N6 and N7, until you come to an easily recognized obelisk on the outskirts of Fontainebleau. The obelisk forms a small island in the middle of a large roundabout which marks the junction where the N6 separates from the N7.

To follow the N6 to Lyon turn to Route Five, page 63. To follow the N7 to the Rhône Valley turn to Route Six, page 67.

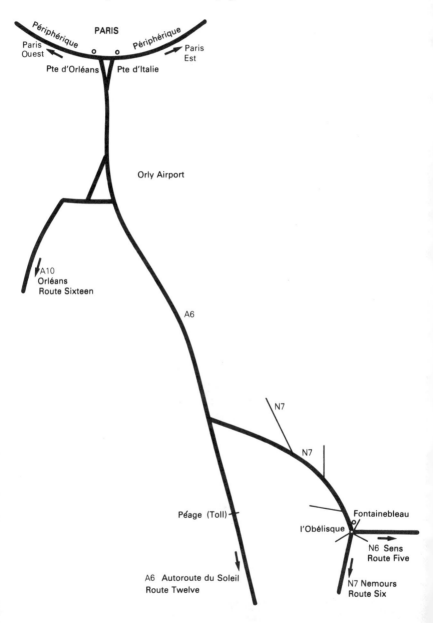

Route Three
Calais — Lyon missing Paris
751km/461mi

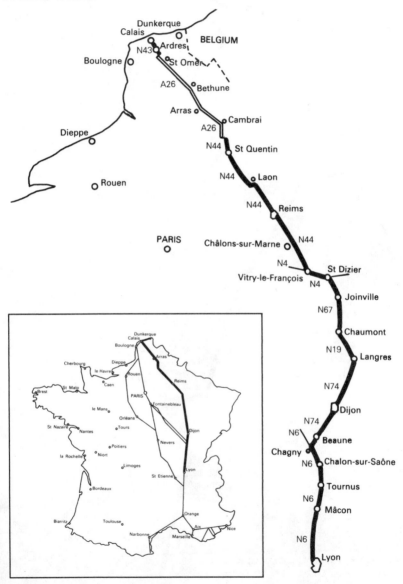

Route Three

Calais — Lyon missing Paris

Leaving the port of Calais, it is very easy to pick up signs for ST OMER. In a matter of a few minutes Calais is left behind, without the need to enter any busy part of the town.

ARDRES

There are 17km/10mi of well-surfaced, two-way road before you turn left in Ardres to skirt the village centre. Then on towards St Omer, through the World War One battlefields marked frequently by the cemeteries of many different nations.

ST OMER

Unless you have reason to visit this busy little town, we suggest you bypass it and the industrial towns, Bethune, Arras and Cambrai, by electing to pay approximately 25F toll and using a 128km/80mi section of motorway.

Before St Omer, take the entrance to the auto-route signed PARIS. Follow this autoroute which will cross over the Autoroute du Nord (Lille — Paris). Continue straight ahead, following the autoroute signed for ST QUENTIN and REIMS.

At the temporary end of the motorway, turn right and follow signs towards ST QUENTIN.

ST QUENTIN

Home of the French bicycle industry, St Quentin can also boast a museum of entomology which claims to hold the world's finest collection of butterflies and insects.

At St Quentin, it is a simple matter to pick up the N44 which is signed for LAON.

LAON

From the 8th to the 10th century it was the capital of France.

Laon (pronounced 'Lahng') is an ancient town built on a hill which rises out of the plains of northern France. It is well worth a visit as it can probably claim to be the most spectacular and most under-publicized town in northern France.

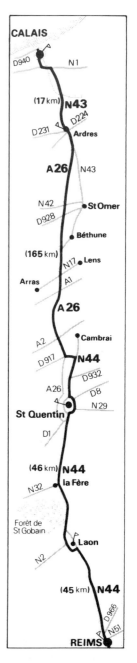

The N44 passes it by and you pick up signs for REIMS. Travel on down the N44 heading for Champagne country, that celebrated but expensive product of Reims.

REIMS
Underneath the city, are miles of galleries housing maturing Champagne. Reims (pronounced 'Rangce') was the site of Eisenhower's H.Q. when he accepted the German surrender in 1945.

Reims is a large city with no bypass from north to south. There is a well-signposted route through the back streets which is easy to follow but requires some concentration — follow signs for CHÂLONS.

Just south of Reims, again on the N44, is the excellent World War One museum at Fort de la Pompelle.

CHÂLONS-SUR-MARNE
Centre of the Champagne vineyards.

Châlons-sur-Marne has a first-class bypass which leads you quickly onto the N44 once more, this time following signs towards VITRY-LE-FRANÇOIS.

VITRY-LE-FRANÇOIS
The beautiful 17th-century church of Notre Dame lies in the impressive Place d'Armes. Leaving Vitry, you turn left onto the N4 (main road Paris — Strasbourg). Follow this busy highway 29km/20mi to ST DIZIER.

ST DIZIER
A famous motor museum at Villiers-en-Lieu.

In the centre of St Dizier, you turn right onto the N67 signed for CHAUMONT. (Be careful — it is easy to miss the turn in St Dizier.)

CHAUMONT
Just west of Chaumont is Colombey-les-Deux-Églises where de Gaulle died and is buried. Chaumont is the centre of the glove-making industry.

Chaumont is a very pleasant town with good hotels and restaurants. Take the N19 towards LANGRES.

LANGRES

This walled city, high on a hill, sits on the hydrographical limit between the North Sea and the Mediterranean. From here on you are in the catchment area which collects all rainfall and feeds it through the Rhône Valley to the Mediterranean.

From Langres, follow the N74 through rolling hills to DIJON.

DIJON

University city famous for its mustard. An ex-Mayor, Canon Kir, gave his name to the famous French drink, kir, which is a mixture of white wine and blackcurrant liqueur.

It is quite easy to follow the N74 round the first-class bypass and emerge following signs for BEAUNE and CHALON-SUR-SAÔNE.

South of Dijon, still on the N74, you pass through the famous Burgundy villages.

BEAUNE

Perhaps the most famous wine centre in the world, now even more well-known as the starting point of the Beaujolais run. It also has a fine museum of the wines of Burgundy.

Follow carefully the signs for CHALON which lead you through the outskirts of Beaune. If you have decided to bypass this pretty town, then be very careful not to be drawn accidentally into the centre: it is an architect's dream and a motorist's nightmare.

CHAGNY

At Chagny join the N6 and follow it south to CHALON-SUR-SAÔNE.

CHALON-SUR-SAÔNE

An important river port, as the Saône is navigable to the Mediterranean via Lyon and the Rhône.

The main through route avoids the town centre. Watch carefully for the right-hand turn to LYON — do not cross the river — leave the town beside the River Saône which heads south on your left-hand side to Tournus.

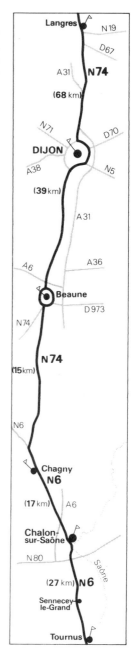

TOURNUS

A town full of antique shops where we have enjoyed good hotels and very good food at most agreeable prices. There is an interesting museum of the history of Burgundy. Follow signs N6 for MÂCON.

MÂCON

Commercial centre of the Burgundy wine industry.

This large industrial city can be bypassed easily by joining the A6 autoroute at the MÂCON-NORD intersection. You simply rejoin the N6 again by leaving the motorway at MÂCON-SUD. There is a special low toll for this stretch of motorway, to encourage long-distance motorists to avoid driving through Mâcon. It is money very well spent.

Those who take the motorway to bypass Mâcon might well decide to stay on it right through to Lyon. It is only a short distance from Mâcon-Sud to where the motorway becomes toll-free at Villefranche.

LYON

See Route Seven page 72 (the Lyon bypass system). From Lyon you may join Route Twelve, the fast route, or Route Eight via the N7.

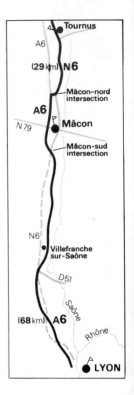

Route Four

Calais — Central France
(missing Paris and linking into
Route Six to miss Lyon)
469km/291mi

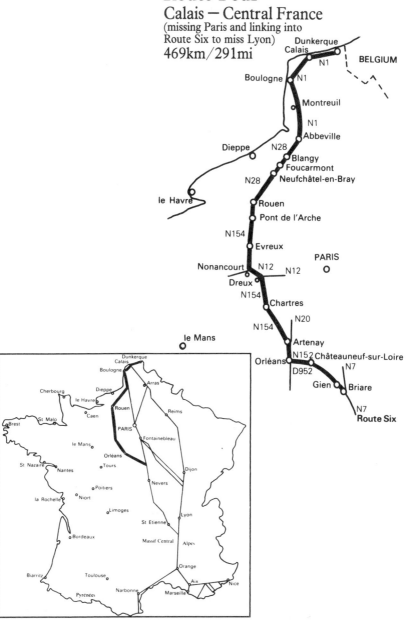

Route Four Calais – Central France missing Paris

This route joins Route Six leading to the Rhône Valley.

CALAIS
When you leave the port, continue 457m/500yds to the roundabout and into Calais through industrial area. Turn right and then left (over canal). Follow carefully signs N1 or RN1 BOULOGNE.

BOULOGNE
The 34km/21mi of uninteresting road from Calais to Boulogne can be avoided by taking a boat from Dover to Boulogne direct at no extra cost.

Leaving Boulogne, watch for signs to PARIS and ABBEVILLE N1. Be careful not to take the road to Le Touquet.

From Boulogne, follow the N1 on south through the vast wheat fields and root crops which are the mainstay of agriculture in northern France. Avenues of trees take the road ahead into the distant rolling hills.

MONTREUIL
Continue to follow the N1 which bypasses the ancient town of Montreuil-sur-Mer with its cobbled streets. Head straight on down the N1, still following signs for ABBEVILLE.

ABBEVILLE
Dropping down the hill into Abbeville, it is a simple matter to spot the signs for ROUEN. Bear to the right at the first roundabout onto a short stretch of the new bypass.

Follow the canal lined with beautiful poplar trees. After 1km/0.63mi, turn right onto the N28 towards ROUEN.

The N28 is a good, very straight road – surely the way the Romans came to Great Britain.

The road at one point twists down into the pretty little town of Blangy, then climbs again.

In the small town of Foucarmont, watch for a sharp turn to the right which you come upon very suddenly.

The N28 continues very straight to Neufchâtel through wooded hills. Follow signs N28 towards ROUEN.

ROUEN

The English burned Joan of Arc here in 1431, but we feel sure the French have forgiven this by now. Chief river port of France.

As you descend the hill into Rouen the view is magnificent with the latticework spire of the cathedral towering out of the centre of the city. Rouen appears to be a vast obstacle in the path of your progress southward. In fact it is very easy to negotiate.

There are two methods of passing through Rouen: there is no true bypass from north to south — just pick up the green signs that first read PARIS and a little further on, PARIS — ORLÉANS. This will feed you into the A13 motorway which you then leave at the first intersection after the city which is signed for EVREUX.

We prefer to follow the signs which read AUTRES DIRECTIONS (other directions) or TOUTES DIRECTIONS (all directions). This sweeps you round to the west of the city on the inner ring road. You pass over the River Seine beside the docks (how do they navigate those ocean-going ships so far inland?). Then immediately after the bridge, you turn sharp left signed ORLÉANS.

On a fine road you follow the river bank eastward for some 3km/2mi following signs for ORLÉANS until it sweeps you back over the river onto the N15, signed ORLÉANS — PARIS.

Follow the N15 signed for EVREUX. Then cross the river again at Pont de l'Arche and drive into beautiful wooded country typical of the Île de France (the Home Counties of France). More than 20 per cent of the population of France lives in the Île de France.

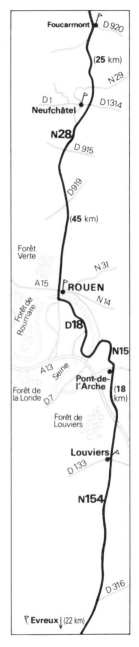

When you arrive at the motorway junction, some care is necessary to pick up and follow signs for EVREUX. From this point, do not pursue signs for Paris: watch always for EVREUX which leads you on down the N154.

EVREUX

A town with many hotels and a good shopping centre. Driving into Evreux, watch for the turning to the left, signed DREUX. The sign reads TOUTES DIRECTIONS and, below it, DREUX.

The bypass is good, signed DREUX all the way straight ahead. At the far end of the bypass, south of the town, turn left again, following the N154, signed DREUX. Then it is a straight 29km/18mi on a good, well-surfaced road (uninteresting). You sweep through agricultural communes where the fields are interspersed with clumps of trees.

Immediately before NONANCOURT, you come onto the junction with the N12, the main road from Paris to Britanny. Turn left, follow the N12 signed DREUX for about 13km/8mi.

DREUX

Pass Dreux, leaving it on your right and continue to use the N12 as a bypass. Then at the far end of the town, turn right. It is signed for CHARTRES. Still on the N154, the road continues again very straight.

At a point some 16km/10mi north of Chartres, you can see the vast form of Chartres cathedral which must surely be one of the most impressive buildings in France. As you drive towards the city, it grows larger and larger until it seems to fill the windscreen.

CHARTRES

Famous for its cathedral and its grain markets.

At the first main junction in the city, the road turns sharp left, signed for ORLÉANS.

Out in the countryside again, the road continues flat, fast and uninteresting until you reach the town of Artenay where you turn right onto the N20 towards ORLÉANS.

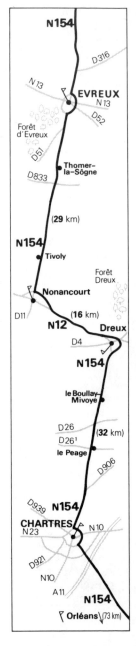

From a point just north of Artenay, right into Orléans, follow the overhead mono-track railway. This impressive concrete gantry carries the experimental hover trains for 48km/30mi in the direction of Paris.

ORLÉANS
Centre of the vinegar industry. Famous for its May festival and the English siege on 8 May, 1429.

As you enter the city, the railway station on your left is a very good landmark, and at this point, watch for signs which take you left to NEVERS.

Following the northern bank of the River Loire you go eastward on the N60 towards CHÂTEAU-NEUF-SUR-LOIRE.

CHÂTEAUNEUF-SUR-LOIRE
In season there are beautiful displays of rhododendrons and azaleas.

This small but interesting town is well blessed with good and inexpensive hotels. Leave the N60 and turn right onto the D952 signed for COSNE.

After Châteauneuf the route becomes much more scenic as you follow the Loire and the D952 to GIEN.

Driving straight through this small town, you head along the river to Briare. The old stone bridge of Gien is a feature of this beautiful town.

BRIARE
Drive straight ahead through the centre of the village. Just after Briare, you join the N7 signed NEVERS. The route from Briare to the Rhône Valley continues on Route Six, page 66.

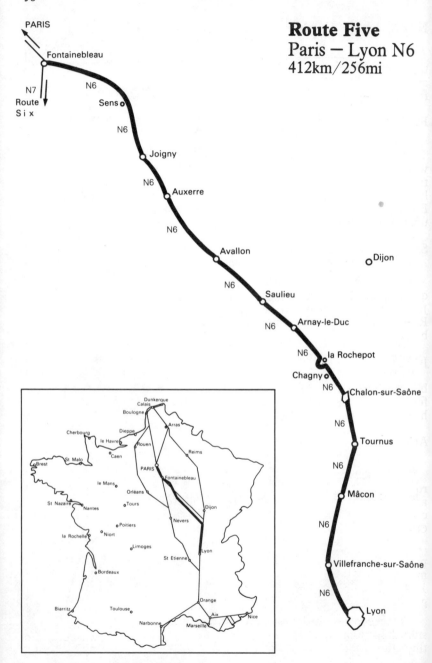

Route Five
Paris – Lyon N6
412km/256mi

PARIS

Fontainebleau

N7
Route
Si x

N6

Sens

N6

Joigny

N6

Auxerre

N6

Avallon

Dijon

N6

Saulieu

N6

Arnay-le-Duc

N6

la Rochepot

Chagny

N6

Chalon-sur-Saône

N6

Tournus

N6

Mâcon

N6

Villefranche-sur-Saône

N6

Lyon

Route Five   Paris — Lyon by the N6

This route starts at the obelisk in the middle of the roundabout at Fontainebleau where the N6 and N7 roads divide. To reach this point, leaving from Paris, see the end of Route Two, page 50.

FONTAINEBLEAU
Napoleon's favourite retreat.

From Fontainebleau the N6 is signed to SENS which you reach after a beautiful drive, first through part of the Forest of Fontainebleau and later through the rolling slopes of the Île-de-France. The countryside then becomes flat and uninteresting just before Sens.

SENS
Thomas à Becket lived here in exile.

There is a very good bypass which takes us quickly past the town. Now follow the N6 towards JOIGNY. The road runs through the valley of the River Yonne with its never-ending stream of barges.

JOIGNY
In Joigny the N6 turns right, over an old stone bridge across the fast-flowing river. Follow signs for AUXERRE. The countryside becomes more hilly.

AUXERRE
One of the oldest towns in France.

Auxerre has no true bypass but the inner relief road, which offers splendid views of the cathedral and abbey, makes it an easy matter to avoid the city centre. Simply follow the signs for AVALLON and CHALON.

The rolling hills south of Auxerre are famous for pottery. There are giant examples of the craftsmen's work at the roadside. One pot stands 4.6m/15ft high and 3.7m/12ft in diameter. A potter's giant masterpiece.

The road follows the River Cousin through limestone hills to the Grottès d'Arcy where you pass through a tunnel to emerge into much hillier coun-

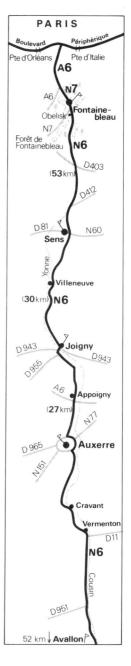

try. The tunnel has poor lighting. The N6 then winds and twists through beautiful hills and a series of pretty villages.

AVALLON
Avallon has no bypass but it is easy to negotiate. Drive straight ahead, following signs for LYON.

You are now heading into the Burgundy region where they have a local proverb: 'Better a good meal than fine clothes'.

SAULIEU
Gastronomic centre of the Morvan.

A little town full of small hotels and restaurants and one of our favourite stopping-off places. Famous for its furniture manufacturers and as a source of Christmas trees.

South of Saulieu, you cross the new high-speed railway line from Paris to Lyon. Soon after this, there is a filling station called Le Petit Train. Here, preserved in the forecourt, there is a little steam train — one extreme to the other.

ARNAY-LE-DUC
Arnay-le-Duc is another of our favourite places for an overnight stop en route to the Mediterranean. Follow the signs for LYON.

From Arnay the road climbs over the hills into Burgundy country, then suddenly descends steeply past the magnificent Château la Rochepot, into a land of vineyards and wine.

CHAGNY
Famous for its full wines from the Côte de Beaune.

Now follow the N6 on south towards CHALON.

CHALON-SUR-SAÔNE
Although the only true bypass round Chalon involves entering and leaving the A6 motorway, it is easy to pass the town centre by a link road and a flyover. Watch carefully for the right-hand turning, signed to LYON. This takes you out of Chalon along the west bank of the River Saône, signed for MÂCON and LYON.

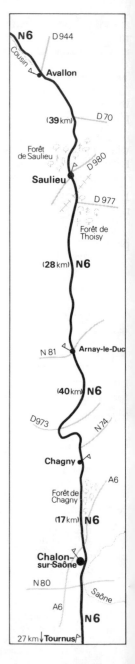

Just south of Chalon, near the road, stands a memorial to French chemist Niepce who invented a process of photography perfected by Daguerre.

TOURNUS

Tournus is an attractive little town, easy to drive through quickly and yet another of our favourite places to spend the night.

The N6 follows the River Saône to MÂCON which is adequately bypassed. Follow signs for LYON.

It is an easy and pleasant drive from Mâcon to Lyon (N6). Views of the Beaujolais hills to the right.

As you approach Lyon, refer to Route Seven on page 72 for the Lyon bypass system.

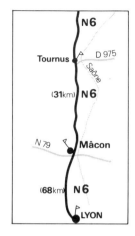

Route Six
Paris — Rhône Valley missing Lyon
540km/335mi

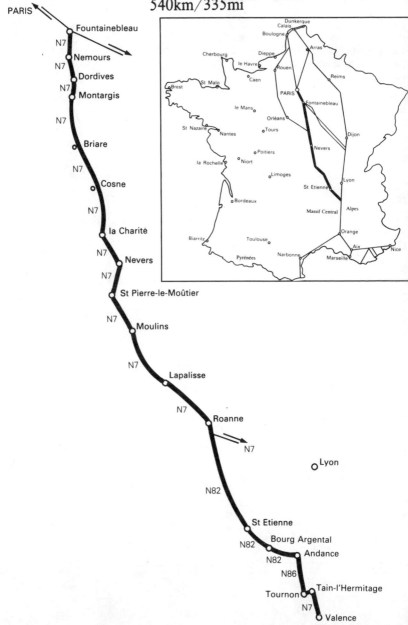

PARIS

Fountainebleau

N7

Nemours

N7

Dordives

N7

Montargis

N7

Briare

N7

Cosne

N7

la Charité

N7

Nevers

N7

St Pierre-le-Moûtier

N7

Moulins

N7

Lapalisse

N7

Roanne

N7

Lyon

N82

St Etienne

N82

Bourg Argental

N82

Andance

N86

Tournon

Tain-l'Hermitage

N7

Valence

Route Six

Paris to the Rhône Valley by the N7 and N82

This route is offered as an alternative to Route Five. It is far more picturesque than travelling by the N6. Be warned, however, that, although it is a very good road throughout its length, it is subject to heavy mist during inclement weather conditions between Fontainebleau and Briare and we do not advise you to use Route Six very early in the morning or between November and April.

The N7 route to Lyon starts at the obelisk in the middle of a roundabout at Fontainebleau where the N6 and N7 divide. To reach this point, leaving from Paris, see Route Two, page 50.

At the obelisk, watch carefully for the sign that reads N7 and NEMOURS.

The road from Fontainebleau to Nemours is very good and passes through an attractive part of the Forest of Fontainebleau.

NEMOURS

Fascinating rock formations surround the town. Nemours is not the easiest of towns to negotiate and it seems to have more than its fair share of heavy vehicles. There is no bypass but there is a fair inner ring road through the suburbs. Follow signs for MONTARGIS.

DORDIVES

The small town of Dordives is quite easy to pass through. Just watch carefully for signs to MONTARGIS.

The road between Dordives and Montargis follows the course of the River Loing and is very prone to heavy mist.

MONTARGIS

After Montargis, a town of water and bridges, the N7 climbs and improves in terms of scenery and road surface as you approach Briare, following signs for NEVERS.

BRIARE

The N7 forms a bypass. You are hardly aware that Briare lies to the right of your road.

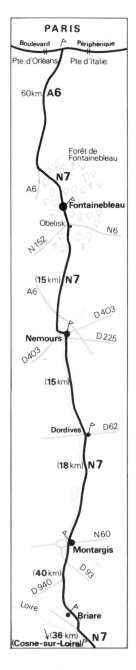

COSNE

A new bypass sweeps you past Cosne and then
on to La Charité where there is a fine stone-built
bridge with eleven impressive arches. We head on
following the N7 towards NEVERS.

NEVERS

St Bernadette lived out her life at the convent.
Her body lies in a glass casket in the chapel.

As you enter Nevers, watch for the sign that
swings you hard left for MOULINS. Then as you
come beside the river, there is another left turn
over the river bridge signed MOULINS – LYON.
Follow the N7 south through the little town of
St Pierre-le-Moûtier, full of small hotels, and on
through rolling hills towards Moulins.

MOULINS

If you are stopping, see the bell tower with
mechanical figures. Driving through Moulins is
enough to make even the most experienced of travellers lose his sense of direction. It consists of so
many turns to the right and to the left that you feel
as though you have driven through a cobweb, but it
is, in fact, quite simple — just concentrate and follow carefully the signs for LYON.

LAPALISSE

South of Moulins, the road is good but uninteresting until suddenly you arrive in the old town of
Lapalisse. Go over the river bridge, turn right and
follow signs for ROANNE and LYON.

Then, abruptly, the countryside changes: beautiful hills give you a taste of things to come as you
leave behind the plains of Northern France, heading for ROANNE.

ROANNE

At times other than the rush hour, it is no problem at all to pass through the city of Roanne. Simply follow signs for LYON as you cross the bridge
over the Loire.

After Roanne, watch carefully for GREEN SIGNS
which lead you right through to the Rhône Valley.

Watch for — and follow — the green arrows. At
the point where the green signs start, continue

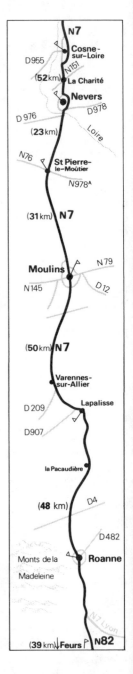

straight ahead on the N82 (the N7 forks left towards Lyon), following green signs and green arrows
which read ST ÉTIENNE and the RHÔNE VALLEY
(Valleé du Rhône).

From this point the road, which remains good,
climbs over the hills towards St Étienne.

ST ÉTIENNE
A large industrial and mining city.

Before entering the city of St Étienne, you pass
over the last few miles of flat, straight road. After
St Étienne, you enter a very different terrain. Follow green arrows. These lead onto a short stretch
of toll-free motorway which is part of the almost
completed bypass for St Étienne. Go right through
and round the city following the green arrows and
green signs towards the RHÔNE VALLEY.

As you climb from the city into the mountains
beyond, the scenery becomes quite spectacular.
When you reach the Col du Grand Bois some
103m/3400ft above sea level, it is difficult to com-
prehend that you have reached an altitude compar-
able to the top of Snowdon.

Follow the green arrows.

BOURG-ARGENTAL
The road through the mountains is a pleasant
and easy drive. Then, still following the green
arrows for the RHÔNE VALLEY, there is a steep descent into Bourg-Argental.

From Bourg-Argental, you climb again — not so
high this time — to the point where, in the middle of
nowhere, you encounter a large roundabout.

Be careful. The green arrows point left towards
Montpellier and Marseille. In fact, it is far better to
go straight on at this roundabout. Follow the signs
for VALENCE.

Within a few hundred yards, you will again find
the green arrows which lead you through beautiful
hills.

As you descend to Andance in the Rhône Valley,
you will be treated to quite spectacular views of the
foothills of the Alps in the distance beyond the
Rhône.

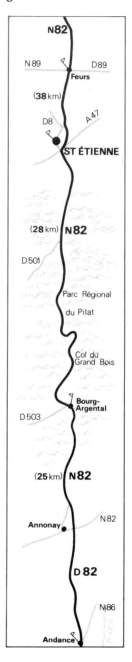

ANDANCE

A tiny village on the banks of the mighty Rhône. Now we fork right and take the N86 as it follows the river towards the Mediterranean.

Still we follow the green signs.

TOURNON

There are fantastic views across the river to the Hermitage Vineyards.

At Tournon, we like to cross the Rhône (leaving the green arrows) to Tain l'Hermitage where, after the bridge, we swing to the right following the east bank of the river.

At this point you rejoin the N7 and Route Eight. See page 75.

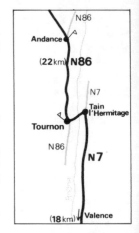

Route Seven
Lyon bypass

Route Seven   The Lyon bypass system

As we said earlier, we make no apology for directing each of Routes One to Twelve through the Rhône Valley. By heading for Lyon and following the Rhône south towards the Mediterranean, you can avoid the mountain roads.

South of Lyon, France becomes very mountainous, with the foothills of the Alps to the east and the Massif Central much nearer, to the west.

Through the two ranges of mountains extending due south from Lyon, runs the majestic valley of the Rhône.

Be alert. You have just covered almost 483km/ 300mi from Paris to Lyon or about one third of the total journey from central England to the Mediterranean. You will find that you have been watching for sign posts to Lyon for so long that it has become a habit. It is, therefore, very easy to find yourself following the Lyon signs right into the city centre. Remember, as soon as you get near the outskirts of Lyon, you must watch for road signs to MARSEILLE.

LYON

Lyon is the third largest city in France and the gastronomical capital of the world. Lyon stands on the junction of two incredible rivers, the Saône and the Rhône. It is the road and rail junction for Switzerland, the Mediterranean and the industrial north — the true centre of France.

THE BYPASS SYSTEM   North to South

You may have arrived at the outskirts of Lyon by way of either the N6, the N7, or the Autoroute du Soleil. On the northern edge of the city, all three roads converge, probably without you really being aware of it. You simply follow signs for MARSEILLE.

Follow the road, which is of motorway standard, into Lyon — always watching for overhead signs to MARSEILLE. The Lyon bypass system is probably one of the best quick-flow systems in Europe. Unless you arrive at rush hour or it is a public holi-

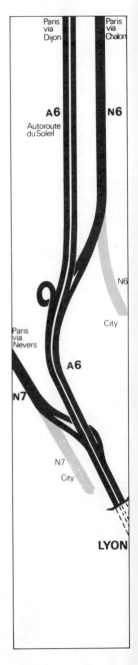

day, you should be clear from north to south of the city in about eight minutes.

The road enters a well-lit and well-ventilated tunnel about 2½km/1½mi long. By law you are required to have dipped headlights.

This tunnel takes you right underneath the northern, hilly, part of the city. You emerge, still on a dual carrriageway, onto the bridge over the River Saône.

Immediately over the bridge, you are faced by the mouths of two parallel tunnels. Take the one under the sign for MARSEILLE.

As you emerge from this much shorter tunnel, the road swings to the right. You are now heading south out of Lyon on the dual carriageway on the west bank of the Rhône.

Within a short distance the road improves from dual carriageway to motorway standard as it sweeps you over the Rhône to the east bank and out of Lyon, past the oil refinery at Feyzin.

It is now not far to the point where you must leave the motorway if you wish to return to the N7. In which case you follow the signs for VIENNE.

Of course, you may elect to stay on the motorway, paying tolls, from here on.

Both routes head down the Rhône Valley crossing and recrossing each other towards the Mediterranean.

See Route Eight page 75 Lyon to Aix-en-Provence by the N7 or Route Twelve page 91 Lyon to Aix-en-Provence by the A7.

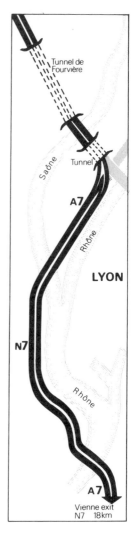

Route Eight
Lyon — Aix-en-Provence
311km/193mi

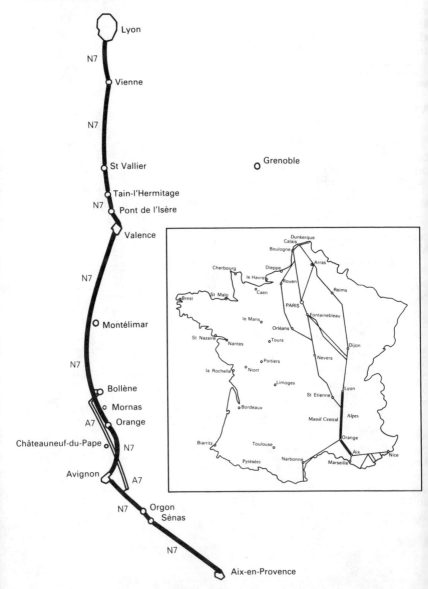

Lyon

N7

Vienne

N7

St Vallier

Tain-l'Hermitage
Pont de l'Isère
N7
Valence

N7

Montélimar

N7

Bollène
Mornas
A7   Orange
Châteauneuf-du-Pape   N7

Avignon   A7

N7   Orgon
Sénas

N7

Aix-en-Provence

Grenoble

Dunkerque
Calais
Boulogne
Arras
Cherbourg   Dieppe
le Havre   Rouen   Reims
St Malo   Caen
Brest   PARIS
le Mans   Fontainebleau
Orléans
St Nazaire   Dijon
Nantes   Tours
Poitiers   Nevers
la Rochelle   Niort
Limoges   Lyon
St Etienne
Bordeaux   Massif Central   Alpes
Biarritz   Toulouse   Orange
Narbonne   Aix   Nice
Pyrénées   Marseille

Route Eight
Lyon — Aix-en-Provence by the N7

The N7 south of Lyon is a toll-free road of motorway standard which sweeps over the fast-flowing Rhône to the east bank. It continues beside the river and remains toll-free for 25km/15mi until just before Vienne.

To avoid entering the toll section of the motorway, you must leave it where VIENNE is signposted.

VIENNE
Famous Roman theatre.

As you leave the motorway, it crosses the Rhône to the west bank, leaving you to enter Vienne right on the edge of the water, following the east bank.

Watch carefully for the sign for a left turn to VALENCE.

Almost immediately (64m/70yds or so), you turn right to head south, out of the town towards Valence.

Follow signs for VALENCE on the N7. This takes you on down the Rhône Valley to St Vallier.

ST VALLIER
At the traffic lights, cross the junction diagonally to take the road beside the river. See the signs for VALENCE. St Vallier is very picturesque, perched as it is on the bank of the river. This is one of the narrowest parts of the valley where the mountains rise steeply on both sides of the Rhône.

The road follows the river closely as the valley widens and, suddenly, the Rhône makes a huge curve to the right extending its width to well over 1km/½mi. This is one of our favourite stopping points. The scenery is magnificent, the river is at its impressive best and you are so aware that the plains and gentle hills of northern France have been left behind.

TAIN L'HERMITAGE
Here we are joined by Route Six. Tain l'Hermitage is a pretty town, famous for its superb wines which are produced from grapes grown on the sides of the steep hills that dominate the town. The vine-

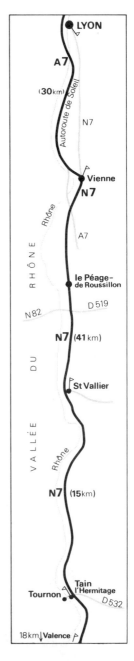

yards are so precariously perched over the town that you feel the grapes could only be harvested by a team of monkeys riding mountain goats!

Follow the N7 straight through the town, taking the signs for VALENCE. North of Valence, you cross the River Isère at the point just before it flows into the Rhône at Pont-de-l'Isère.

VALENCE
At the approach to Valence you have the opportunity to miss the town by taking the bypass — signed for AVIGNON — which sweeps you round the west of the town. It rejoins the N7 some 6km/4mi south of the centre of Valence.

Heading on south the N7 crosses the Drôme, another of the rivers which, in spring, carry the melting snow from the Alps into the Rhône.

The N7 heads on south towards MONTÉLIMAR.

MONTÉLIMAR
Famous for its nougat.

At the entry to the town the bypass is a turning to the right signed for AVIGNON. Take it. You will emerge on the N7 south of the town — a really worthwhile diversion which avoids the traffic congestion of Montélimar.

Between Montélimar and Avignon, you enter Provence and at any time of the year, you may expect a very dramatic improvement in weather conditions. We have travelled this stretch of road many times and it has never failed to produce a sudden and exhilarating change in climate.

South of Montélimar, the N7 passes the outskirts of the 11th-century village of Mornas which snuggles into the base of a cliff while above the town, man-made cave dwellings in the cliff face which date back to a much earlier period can be seen.

AVOIDING ORANGE, AVIGNON
Heading on south, you now come to the Roman town of Orange, which vies with Avignon to be the most difficult town to negotiate along the length of the N7. There is no bypass but you can join the motorway north of the town at Bollène following the blue signs to ORANGE and MARSEILLE and leave it to rejoin the N7 at Avignon South. We think it is

well worth using this stretch of motorway.

ORANGE

The fantastic Roman remains in Orange include the original Arc de Triomphe and one of the largest Roman theatres in France. The town is an historian's dream and a driver's nightmare.

Just south of Orange, only 5km/3mi off the N7 is the famous wine-producing village of Châteauneuf-du-Pape.

Driving through Orange, again follow signs for AVIGNON — the next major point on the route.

AVIGNON

Some may wish to visit the ruined bridge from the song everyone learned at school 'Sur le Pont d'Avignon'.

Following the signs for AIX-EN-PROVENCE (some signposts just point to AIX), we normally head away from the city out into the countryside where we can enjoy the Provençal sunshine.

As you leave Avignon, you will see the first signpost that reads NICE. Driving on south, you become aware of signs of change in the vegetation and the magnificent scenery. It is a really beautiful setting in which to find an occasional orange tree and orchards of peaches.

At the village of Orgon, the N7 runs close to the Durance — in summer it is just a trickle of water through a very wide river bed.

SÉNAS

At Sénas, watch for the left turn (really a fork) towards AIX-EN-PROVENCE. The last 48km/30mi is through scenery that becomes more and more Provençal until the N7 feeds into the Aix bypass. You now follow Route Nine or Route Ten for destinations on the Côte d'Azur.

Route Nine
Aix — Cannes
　　— Antibes
　　— Nice
　　— Villefranche
　　— Monte Carlo
　　— Menton

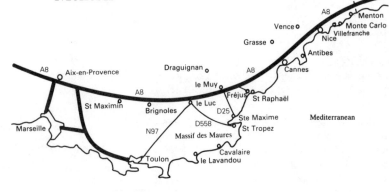

Route Nine   Aix to Cannes, Antibes, Nice, Villefranche, Monte Carlo, Menton

The Aix-en-Provence bypass to which you are directed in Route Eight feeds directly onto the A8 motorway towards NICE, known as La Provençale. Some care is necessary to avoid taking the southbound motorway to Marseille.

La Provençale runs roughly parallel with the sea, right through to the Italian border which is beyond Menton. It is the easiest and smoothest-flowing route from Aix to Nice.

It also runs parallel to the Route Nationale Sept (N7) for most of its distance. The N7 can, however, be very crowded with holiday traffic in season.

The tolls are something like 25 per cent more expensive on La Provençale than on the Autoroute du Soleil but it is an incredible piece of civil engineering. The stretch from Nice to Menton is really spectacular and, to some, even so frightening that it is becoming a tourist attraction in its own right! A series of tunnels and viaducts cross at four hundred feet above the valley, following an 'impossible' path through the lower slopes of the Maritime Alps to the Italian border.

AIX-EN-PROVENCE TO CANNES, ANTIBES, NICE, VILLEFRANCHE, MONTE CARLO AND MENTON

If you are driving to any one of these towns, we advise you to take the A8 motorway from Aix-en-Provence right through to the exit point nearest to your destination. In each case the exit from the motorway is clearly marked.

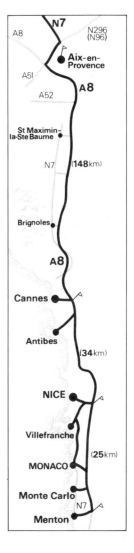

Route Ten

Aix — Fréjus
  — St Raphaël
  — St Aygulf
  — Agay
  — Cassis
  — la Ciotat
  — Bandol
  — Sanary
  — Toulon

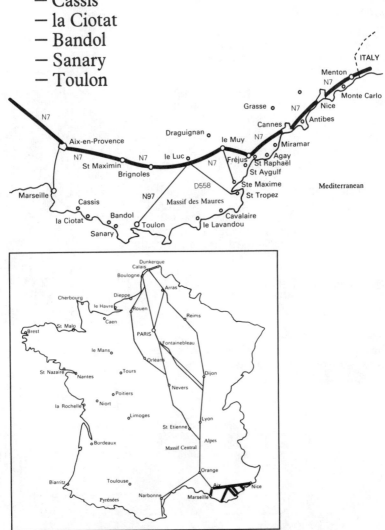

Route Ten   Aix to Fréjus, St Raphaël, St Aygulf, Agay, Cassis, La Ciotat, Bandol, Sanary, Toulon

Aix-en-Provence is less than 32km/20mi from the Mediterranean. (You can drive to the sea at Marseille by motorway in 15 minutes or so, but it is unlikely that you would choose Marseille with its vast docks and heavy industry as your preferred destination for a holiday.)

From Aix you can take either the N7 or A8 motorway known as La Provençale for which tolls are roughly 25 per cent more expensive than for the Autoroute du Soleil but it is an incredible feat of engineering. Both roads pursue an eastward course roughly parallel to the sea and each other. Take care in selecting the point at which you leave these fine highways for the short drive to the coast.

Although the N7 and A8 follow the line of the coast, you must first cross a range of mountains to reach the sea.

As you leave Aix, the Massif de la Sainte Baume separates you from Cassis, La Ciotat, Bandol, Sanary and the city of Toulon, denying you easy access.

The Massif des Maures lies between the roads and Le Lavandou, Cavalaire, St Tropez, Ste Maxime and St Aygulf.

There is a gap in the mountains through the Plain of Fréjus which allows easy access to St Raphaël and Fréjus itself.

The red rocky crags of the Massif de l'Esterel cut off Agay and Miramar before the N7 drops down to the sea.

Each of these mountain ranges affords magnificent views and they are well worth exploring during your holiday but, for the moment, we will assume that you simply want to find the easiest way to reach your destination. One of the following four short routes will enable you to do this, travelling from Aix-en-Provence.

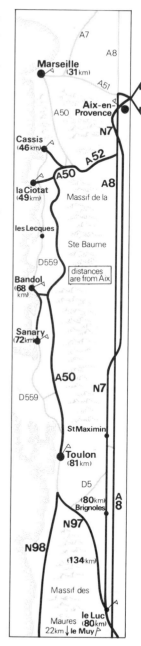

AIX-EN-PROVENCE TO CASSIS, LA CIOTAT, BANDOL, SANARY, TOULON

We believe the best and easiest route to each of these towns is by motorway. Leave Aix-en-Provence by La Provençale autoroute, signed NICE. Just after the toll gates, take the motorway for TOULON. This swings you due south towards the coast. You simply stay in the lane under the overhead sign TOULON.

The exits for CASSIS, LA CIOTAT, BANDOL and SANARY are clearly marked along the autoroute. In each case, when you leave the autoroute you have only a short drive to your destination.

AIX-EN-PROVENCE TO LE LAVANDOU

Without doubt, this is the most difficult coastal resort to reach as it is tucked away on the coast at a point central to the Massif des Maures. All the access routes have differing problems. Do not be tempted to try the mountain roads which appear to lead direct from the N7 to Le Lavandou. After many hours of testing various routes we have decided that the easiest way is to follow the N7 to LE LUC. Turn right onto the N97 signed TOULON. Follow it through and onto the motorway. Leave the motorway at the first exit signed HYÈRES. Bypass Hyères following signs to LAVANDOU.

AIX-EN-PROVENCE TO ST TROPEZ, STE MAXIME, CAVALAIRE

From Aix-en-Provence, continue east on either the N7 or the parallel motorway La Provençale. The N7 offers a pleasant drive through St Maxime, Brignoles and Le Luc.

Do not follow signposts to the south from Le Luc on the D558 to St Tropez. It is a difficult and congested mountain road.

Continue on the N7 or La Provençale motorway to a point approaching LE MUY (pronounced 'Mwee'). From Le Muy take the excellent D25 over the Maures to STE MAXIME.

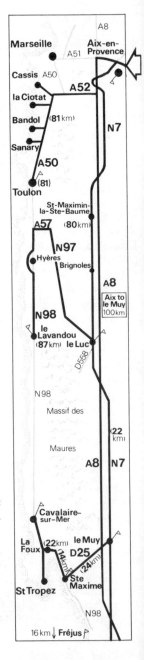

From Ste Maxime you double back along the coast road for the last 8km/5mi to LA FOUX and the turning onto the ST TROPEZ PENINSULA.

To reach Cavalaire, continue straight ahead at La Foux on the D559 through La Croix-Valmer.

AIX-EN-PROVENCE TO FRÉJUS, ST RAPHAËL, ST AYGULF AND AGAY

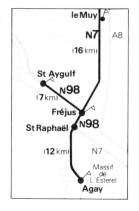

From Aix the N7 runs east and passes through both Fréjus and St Raphaël, which are adjoining towns.

For St Aygulf, enter Fréjus and follow the coast road signed for STE MAXIME. It is only 6km/4mi to St Aygulf.

For Agay, continue through Fréjus into St Raphaël and then watch very carefully for signs to L'ESTÉREL and AGAY.

Route Eleven
Orange — Narbonne and the Spanish Frontier
392km/243mi

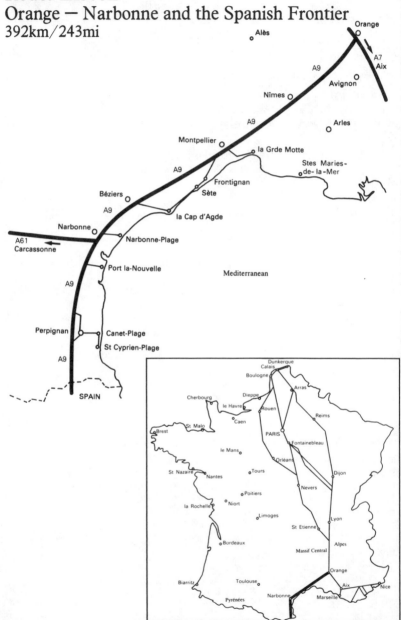

Route Eleven   Towards the Spanish Border

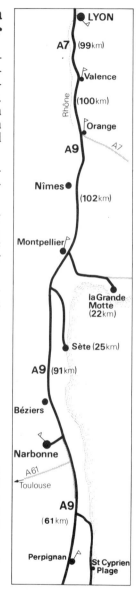

The Mediterranean coast of France from Marseille to the frontier with Spain has been the beneficiary of massive government investment in successive attempts to turn it into a second Côte d'Azur. Although, in our opinion, these have not been entirely successful, the Languedoc-Roussillon coast does offer superb beaches and the hinterland is a maze of interesting towns and villages.

We strongly advise those wishing to reach a destination on this stretch of coast to use the Languedocienne motorway from just north of Orange.

You can reach Orange from Lyon either by Route Twelve — The Fast Route by motorway, page 85, or by Route Eight, page 69. Before Orange, take the A9 motorway which is signed for ESPAGNE — REMOULINS — NARBONNE.

It is then simply a case of following the motorway down the coast and watching for the exit signs to your destination.

FOR LA GRANDE MOTTE
Leave the motorway at MONTPELLIER EST.

FOR SÈTE
Leave the motorway at MONTPELLIER SUD.

NARBONNE
Follow the signs off the motorway.

SIGEAN — LEUCATE (LES ETANGS)
The Etangs are salt water lakes which are separated from the Mediterranean Sea by a ribbon of sand which varies in width from just 100 metres to two kilometres. This stretch of sand runs from Port la Nouvelle to Canet Plage and contains some of the best beaches in the South of France.

If you are heading on into Spain continue on the A9 motorway signed ESPAGNE.

Route Twelve
Calais — Nice by motorway
1221km/757mi

Route Twelve

The Fast Route
Calais — Nice by motorway

As a young man, before the motorway system through France was constructed, I drove single-handed from London to St Tropez in 20 hours. In 1983 when domestic circumstances forced us to return home from the Côte d'Azur as quickly as possible, we left St Tropez at 6.15am and drew up at the port of Calais at 6pm. We arrived home at Newport Pagnell at 11pm. Never would we wish to make such a journey again. We covered 1416km/880mi in $17\frac{3}{4}$ hours at an average speed of 80kmph or 50mph including all stops and the time taken for the ferry crossing. On both occasions it took two whole days to recover from the journey.

When we talk now of the 'Fast Route', we refer only to our suggested itinerary. It must be for the individual to decide at what time he wishes to enter and leave his motor cell and how much of each day he wishes to spend in the driving seat.

It is possible, from wherever you live in England or Wales, to drive comfortably to the South of France with only one night spent en route. Although it is very easy for those who live on the French side of London, it must be accepted that the further north you live, the more difficult it becomes and for the Scots, unfortunately, it is virtually impossible.

Increasing distance is not the only problem: the time taken to cross London is a major factor. If you can make a really early start from home, traverse London and be on the M2 Dover road by 7am, then the time taken from the north to the south of London may only be half an hour. Try the same journey half an hour later and you may well add on an hour and a half or perhaps two hours. (When the M25 round London has been completed, this part of the journey will be less of a problem.)

When you are aiming to get to the sun quickly, the journey should surely be undertaken in a manner which, as far as possible, makes the trip an enjoyable part of the holiday. There is no sense at all in arriving at the Mediterranean in a state of total fatigue. This will simply mean wasting two valuable days of your holiday recovering from the journey.

When we journey from Newport Pagnell in the south Midlands, we like to pack everything into our car the night before departure and go to bed early. Getting up at 4.30am is no real hardship when going on holiday and at 5am we are in the car and rolling.

We head south on the M1 and leave London city behind us before it wakes up. Always driving at the legal limit, we know we will be at Dover Eastern Docks before 7.30am. An early ferry is essential to our plan. We like to take an 8am boat from Dover.

With a sea crossing of 1 hour 30 minutes plus a time difference of one hour, we expect to be driving out of Calais or Boulogne at 11 am.

We make it a hard and fast rule on day one that wherever we are at 6pm, we stop serious travelling and look for a hotel for the night. By 6.30pm you will find us unwinding as we sip a pastis at the bar of our hotel, probably about halfway between Paris and Lyon. Then we have a leisurely bath before dinner. That first meal in France always seems to be the best of the holiday. Then it's early to bed — tired, but usually very pleased with the distance covered and fresh enough for a second early start on day two.

From long experience we find that by spending one night en route, we can arrive at St Tropez in mid-afternoon on the second day of our journey. We can arrive relaxed, not over tired and in good time to spend a couple of hours on the beach. It is very rewarding to lie in the Mediterranean sun, knowing that you left home only yesterday morning.

THE ROUTE
Our fast route to the Côte d'Azur is as follows:
FERRY: DOVER — CALAIS OR BOULOGNE (then head for)
        ST OMER
        A26 AUTOROUTE — ARRAS
        A1 AUTOROUTE
        PARIS
        A6 AUTOROUTE
        LYON
        A7 AUTOROUTE
        AIX-EN-PROVENCE
        LA PROVENÇALE AUTOROUTE
        TOWARDS NICE AND YOUR SELECTED DESTINATION

Apart from the first few miles from Calais to the autoroute, this route is of motorway standard all the way. Neither the Périphérique, which is the Paris ring road, nor the tunnel bypass systems at Lyon are motorways but both are first class and can be regarded as equal to them.

You pay tolls to use French motorways and they are not cheap but in our experience when driving a family car, there is usually a small saving in using the autoroutes and paying tolls as opposed to spending a second night at a hotel en route. See table of tolls page 28.

CHANNEL PORTS — PARIS

N43 from the port of Calais — watch carefully for signs to ST OMER (N42 from Boulogne — watch carefully for signs to ST OMER). Since Calais opened its new car ferry terminal with its improved access road, the route to St Omer is very easy to pick up and follow.

N43 between Ardres and St Omer — watch for the blue motorway signs. Take the A26 autoroute signed for Paris.

Entering and leaving French autoroutes can be difficult with right-hand drive cars when travelling alone. The pay boxes or automatic ticket dispensers are, of course, on the wrong side of the car. When alone, this tricky operation takes time and for those of us who are not so agile it is sometimes easier to get out of the car and walk quickly to the other side.

The first short stretch the A26 motorway forms part of the spur road which will soon (around 1987) be open right through to Calais. After the junction for ARRAS NORTH (Nord), you join the main A1 motorway (Autoroute du Nord) and start to head due south towards Paris through the battlefields of the Somme.

After passing the toll booth near Senlis, continue south, still on the A1, heading for PARIS. There are no more tolls until you are 48km/30mi south of Paris.

Shortly, the autoroute passes under the runways of the Charles de Gaulle Airport. This is an important landmark — an aid to route finding. Immediately after the airport, watch for the slip road, to the right, signed ORLÉANS and LYON — take it. This leads you onto a motorway link road which bypasses all of north east Paris. (If you miss this turn or wish to enter Paris, see Route Two, Paris Ring Road page 49.)

You then emerge onto the Paris ring road (Périphérique) at Porte de Bagnolet.

PÉRIPHÉRIQUE

Follow the Périphérique in the direction signed SUD and LYON. (Each exit from the Périphérique is named as follows: Porte de Bagnolet, Porte de Montreuil, Port de Vincennes etc. For more details, see Route Two.) At each exit, the name of

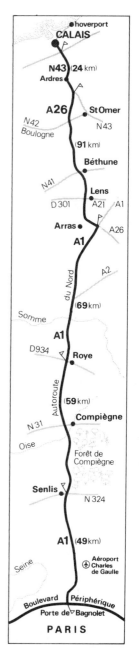

the next is clearly shown on a sign above the road. The exit is on the right.

Watch for signs to LYON.

The A6 Lyon exit is between Porte d'Italie and Porte d'Orléans — take up the nearside (right-hand lane) before reaching the exit point.

A6 PARIS — LYON

As you head off the Périphérique onto the autoroute, there lies ahead of you 448km/278mi of motorway straight down the centre of France to Lyon.

As long as you are going straight through to Lyon, you need not give any thought to navigation at any point during this long stretch of road. It is simply a question of pushing on and watching as the distance to Lyon steadily drops. A sensible drive will put 100km/62mi behind you in each hour of driving.

We like to make our overnight stop somewhere in this section between Paris and Lyon. Paris to Lyon is a long stretch and it always seems so much easier to cover about half in one day and the balance the following morning.

We usually leave the autoroute at the junction for AVALLON. This emerges onto the Route Nationale Six (N6) just south of Avallon. We follow the N6 south to either Saulieu or Arnay-le-Duc. Both small towns offer a selection of clean, low-priced hotels and restaurants.

Next morning, usually starting at about 7.30am, we head on south down the N6 and rejoin the autoroute at Chalon-sur-Saône.

Heading on down the A6 Autoroute du Soleil (Sunshine Motorway), Lyon is now only one and a quarter hours ahead.

The toll gate at the southern end of the A6 is situated at Villefranche, some 32km/20mi north of Lyon. The motorway is then free of tolls until you reach a point about 19km/12mi south of Lyon.

LYON BYPASS

Follow the motorway into Lyon. It is important

to watch for overhead signs to MARSEILLE.

The Lyon bypass system is probably the best and simplest in Europe. Unless you arrive at the rush hour, you should be clear through the third largest city in France in about eight minutes.

The A6 motorway from the north takes you into a well-lit tunnel (you require dipped headlights by law) which takes you for 2½km/1½mi under the northern part of the city.

When you emerge from the long tunnel, there is a straight stretch of road only 183m/200yds long as you cross the River Saône.

Ahead of you are the entrances to two parallel tunnels — Take the one under the overhead sign MARSEILLE.

The exit from this short tunnel swings you to the right and along a dual carriageway of motorway standard which is built right on the banks of the Rhône. This leads directly onto the Autoroute du Soleil which heads south, roughly following the curve of the Rhône towards the Mediterranean.

LYON — AIX-EN-PROVENCE A7

The motorway crosses and recrosses the Rhône at Vienne before you reach the toll gates at Le Péage-de-Roussillon.

Heading on south down the Rhône Valley, the autoroute bypasses Valence and Montélimar, before which you will spot that magical sign beside the road that reads 'Vous êtes en Provence'. Now you can expect not only changes in scenery and vegetation but also a rapid improvement in temperature as you head on south to Montélimar and Bollène.

On the A7 before Orange, is the junction with the A9 motorway, signed ESPAGNE – REMOULINS – NARBONNE, the route for those heading to south west France and the Spanish border. Page 78, Route 11.

The A7 continues past Carpentras and Avignon to the toll gate at Salon.

Soon after the toll gate, there is a second toll booth where payment of 5F is the only sign that

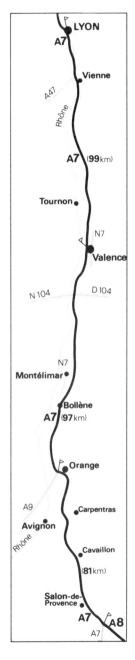

you have left the Autoroute du Soleil and entered a new autoroute called La Provençale.

LA PROVENÇALE — A8

Only a short distance after this second toll booth, you must be prepared for the fork in the motorway NICE — MARSEILLES.

Follow the sign for NICE, in the direction of Aix-en-Provence. As the motorway bypasses Aix-en-Provence, continue to follow signs for NICE on the A8.

Travelling east from Aix, you soon reach the first toll gate. The motorway then runs parallel to the Mediterranean right through to the Italian border.

Where you leave the autoroute for the short drive down to the sea will, of course, depend on your eventual destination. See Routes Nine and Ten to the Côte D'Azur.

Route Napoléon
Cannes — Tournus
500km/310mi

One year after his defeat by the allied armies the Emperor Napoléon returned secretly to France from exile on the Isle of Elba. He landed at Golfe-Juan at 5pm on March 1st 1815. His aim was to march to Paris and regain control of France. He stated that his emblem, the eagle, would fly from steeple to steeple until it reached the towers of Notre Dame.

The N85 road which follows closely the path used by the Emperor was opened in 1933. Inevitably named the Route Napoléon it is marked throughout by the sign of the eagle which will be seen at the entrance of each village along the way.

Warning
In winter this route is subject to heavy snowfalls. Between November and April the passes are frequently closed.

NB Those following the Route Napoléon in the reverse direction should leave Tournus by crossing the river bridge signed BOURG. Then follow the route watching carefully for signs to each town on the route. When leaving Grenoble you should not take the road signed to Gap and Digne. You require the more local sign into the suburb of EYBENS. From Eybens head south to VIZILLE.

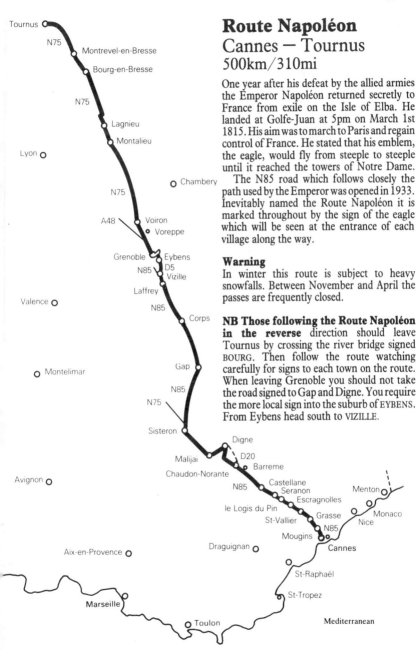

Route Napoléon   Cannes — Grenoble and to the A6 & N6 at Tournus

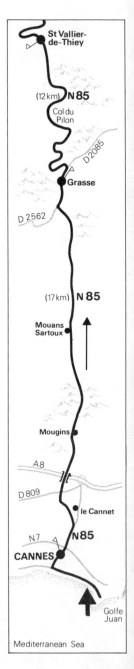

CANNES

We pick up the Route Napoléon by following the expressway (Boulevard d'Alsace) which runs through Cannes parallel to the sea front. It does not matter if you enter Cannes from the east or the west. Those who cling to the seafront and use the Boulevard de la Croisette will need to turn away from the sea, and into the town, to pick up the Boulevard d'Alsace.

From Boulevard d'Alsace turn north into Boulevard Carnot at the junction signed LE CANNET GRASSE AUTOROUTE. As you pass the town sign for le Cannet you will see under it the first sign bearing the eagle of Napoléon.

LE CANNET

Immediately after the town sign, still in Boulevard Carnot, watch carefully for overhead signs MOUGINS PAR N85 — these will take you left into Boulevard Paul Doumer. As the road climbs through the outskirts of le Cannet watch for the MOUGINS GRASSE sign at traffic lights leading right into Avenue Franklin Roosevelt. Follow signs for GRASSE — cross straight over the D809.

MOUGINS

As you enter Mougins — sadly the eagle is missing — you climb through the village into Val de Mougins and ahead you see the mountains that lie in your path.

GRASSE

On the climb to Grasse the eagle takes the form of a most strange piece of graphic artistry. Grasse is famous as the home of the French perfume industry and it is also the headquarters of the Route Napoléon Society, Place de la Foux. 06130 Grasse. Tel: (93) 36.03.56.

Follow the signs for CENTRE VILLE and then pick up signs for DIGNE. (There is an inner ring road but usually it is more congested than the town centre.)

From Grasse you climb steeply to the pass of Col du Pilon 786m (2578ft). There are quite splendid views back over the Esterel Coast and eastward towards Monaco and the Italian frontier. There is also a pilot's eye view of the runway on the airfield at Mandelieu.

As you follow the road deeper into the mountains there are superb views to the west of the hills of Roquebrune, the Maures and the lake of St Cassien before the descent into St Vallier.

ST VALLIER-de-THIEY

The route winds straight through the town. After St Vallier the road climbs again to the Pas de la Faye 981m (3218ft). Follow signs for CASTELLANE and DIGNE (N85).

ESCRAGNOLLES

The road descends steeply from the village perched on the edge of the mountains. Then the road climbs yet again to the Col de Valferrière 1169m (3805ft) and on the following descent the scenery is no longer of the Cote d'Azur, the air is colder and the scenery reminiscent of Switzerland. Continue to follow N85 signs to CASTELLANE.

SERANON

A sleepy village where Napoléon spent the night of March 2nd in the Castle of the Marquess of Gourdon, mayor of Grasse.

LE LOGIS DU PIN

We pass through pine forests at the junction of Var and Alpe Maritime and we continue to follow signs for CASTELLANE as we drive into Alpes — Haute-Provence.

The fourth climb to the Col de Luens 1054m (3467ft) is followed by the long run down into Castellane.

CASTELLANE

The town is a real tourist centre situated at the head of the Gorge du Verdon. (Well worth a visit, it is said to be the second largest canyon in the world.) The town is dominated by a gigantic column of limestone on top of which is perched a chapel. Our route takes us over the River Verdon into the town square where we turn right following the signs to DIGNE.

After Castellane the road climbs steeply again. Only minutes after leaving the town it is a dinky model far below. The Col de Leques is 1146m (3596ft). Then comes the rapid drop down through the rugged cliffs and crazy rock formations of the Clue de Taulanne. We pass Senez to our left and weird pinnacles of rock to our right.

CHAUDON-NORANTE

At Chaudon-Norante the modern Route Napoléon leaves the path followed by the Emperor. (The historical route follows roughly the line of the D20 over the Col du Corobin. It is a hard and tortuous route best left to historians and adventurers.) Continue to follow the N85 signed DIGNE.

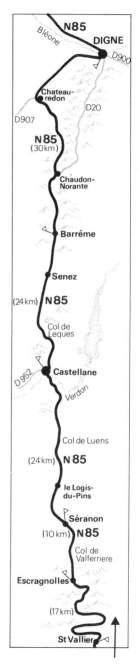

DIGNE

This is a beautiful spa town with very good hotels and restaurants.

Cross the river and follow green signs to SISTERON and GRENOBLE N85.

The road from Digne to Sisteron is level and a fast flowing road of RN standard. It rushes through Malijai, where Napoléon spent the night at the chateaux, then it sweeps across the River Durance, a crossing which caused Napoléon considerable problems and forced him to take several diversions.

We follow the River Durance north as it flows through a series of barrages and giant sluice gates. Soon ahead of us we can see the hill top fort strategically situated to defend the gorge at Sisteron.

SISTERON

The town is built in tiers on the slopes of the hill which is topped by the citadel. A tunnel permits the N85 to avoid the congestion of the town centre.

Follow signs for GRENOBLE. As you leave the town the road swings right to cross the Buech just before it joins the Durance.

Be careful. After 3.5km there is a fork signed GAP. Stay on the N85. Do not take the N75 which is signed with green arrows to Grenoble and Lyon. The N85 is much improved north of Sisteron and runs through beautiful mountains without requiring that you climb them. Superb views of distant snow-capped peaks even in July and August.

GAP

At an altitude of 735m Gap is an attractive winter sports centre. There is an Olympic skating rink. Ten ski centres lie within 40km and the cross-country ski resort at Bayard is nearby.

Follow green signs for GRENOBLE. The road climbs over the Col Bayard 1246m then a long easy descent to la Fare where Napoléon was joyously received by the locals but refused to take their menfolk into his army.

At the entrance to Corps there is an attractive roadside picnic spot and viewpoint looking out from high above the lake.

CORPS

Napoléon stayed the night in this little town perched above the lake. We doubt if he was 'ripped off' as modern day tourists are. We paid more for a beer than we expect to pay in St Tropez. We looked at the menus at several restaurants and quickly went back to the Route Napoléon.

The N85 continues northward through more wooded countryside passing through several small villages all proudly displaying the sign of the eagle. Lovely views.

LAFFREY

It was here that Napoléon came face to face with the king's troops sent from Grenoble to intercept him. There is a fine statue of the Emperor on horseback at the spot which is known as the *'Prairie de la Rencontre'* (The meadow of the meeting). The two armies joined forces and together set off on the trek to Grenoble.

NB Immediately after the meadow of the meeting comes the very steep and dangerous descent to Vizille. No coaches, lorries or caravans are permitted on this road. Watch for well-signed diversions.

Warning. The road descends very steeply through trees towards Vizille in the valley below. At the foot of the hill the road is signed N85 GRENOBLE. This takes you down a slip road onto a new by-pass which rushes you quickly north into the outskirts of Grenoble. If you take that road you have seen your last eagle. To continue along the Route Napoléon you must go straight ahead into Vizille.

VIZILLE

Continue straight into the town, bear left in the square and continue straight ahead following the D5.

You will see the eagle again at Brie and at Tavernolle before descending through pretty hills with views of Grenoble ahead in the distance.

EYBENS

Eybens is the last place on the Route Napoléon where you will see the sign of the eagle. Sadly we could find no trace of the emblem on the town limits of Grenoble.

GRENOBLE
Follow the blue signs for LYON and take the motorway out of the city. (There is no toll payment required for the first stretch of motorway).

Leave motorway at Voreppe signed VOIRON LYON par RN BOURG-EN-BRESSE.

Follow signs for BOURG (after leaving the motorway there is a short link road before you join the N75 signed BOURG.)

VOIRON
It is here that the famous green Chartreuse liqueur is made. In the Boulevard Edger-Kofler you can visit the caves and watch part of the process. Not open at weekends. No visitors are received at the monastery which is some distance away in the Chartreuse Hills.

Follow green signs BOURG-EN-BRESSE.

LAGNIEU
Follow the main road into town, turn right at T junction in centre and follow signs for BOURG.

In open countryside the N75 and N84 converge — follow signs for BOURG — shortly afterwards the two roads divide again and go their separate ways — the junction is a little complicated — just follow signs for BOURG.

It is possible to by-pass Bourg-en-Bresse by using a short stretch of the A40 motorway which has been constructed for this purpose.

Those electing to miss the town will join the N975 north of Bourg.

BOURG-EN-BRESSE
At Brou in the south east of the town, off the N75 to your right, is one of the most splendidly flamboyant gothic churches ever built. It is well worth a visit.

North of Bourg-en-Bresse the N75 becomes the N975 and runs through some pretty villages in an area renowned for its dairy produce. Follow signs first for MONTREVEL then TOURNUS.

TOURNUS
The N975 enters the town by the bridge over the River Saône. It is a simple matter to pick up our Routes. **Route Five** — turn right onto the N6, or **Route Twelve** — Join the Autoroute A6 signed PARIS.

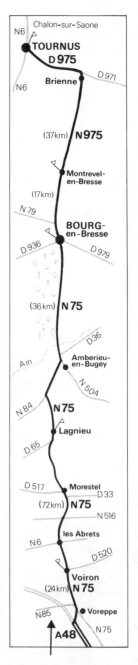

Route Thirteen
Dieppe — Poitiers
420km/260mi

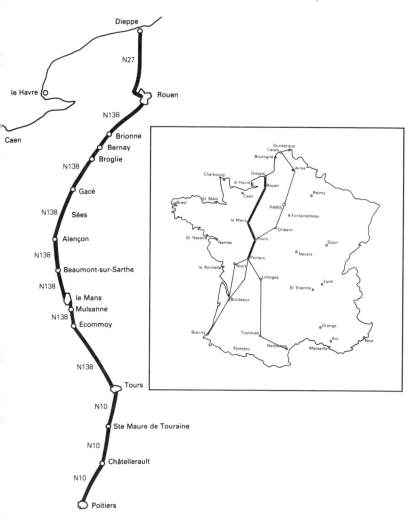

Route Thirteen   Dieppe — Poitiers

DIEPPE

Dieppe claims to be the oldest seaside resort in France.

Ferries docking at Dieppe tie up in a pool right in the centre of the old town itself. It is a very impressive first look into the everyday life of France.

When you drive from the ferry, following the quay to customs and passport control, you pass from the town centre to emerge onto French roads along the esplanade which fronts the sea.

Drive straight ahead for the full length of the sea front. At the far end, the road turns sharp left under the walls of the castle dominating the cliff in front of you. Follow signs PARIS — ROUEN.

Go straight ahead past traffic lights, continuing up the hill.

Watch for the fork to Paris and Rouen. You require the right fork for ROUEN. Follow the N27.

At a point 16km/10mi before Rouen, you have the choice of continuing on the N27 or taking to the motorway. Take the motorway: it is toll-free and you will enter Rouen by a much easier route.

ROUEN

A substantial commercial port, despite lying 64km/40mi from the sea, on the Seine. Rouen abounds with fine museums and visitors will be drawn to the great clock and the site where Joan of Arc was executed in 1431.

When the motorway ends, you will find yourself almost immediately on the cobbles of the dock area. Follow the green overhead signs, TOUTES DIRECTIONS.

The next overhead sign is blue — PARIS. Follow it up the slip road which then swings right, over the Seine bridge.

From the bridge, your route is straight ahead, watching carefully for the green signs to ALENÇON on the N138.

BRIONNE

The road winds its way downhill into the town.

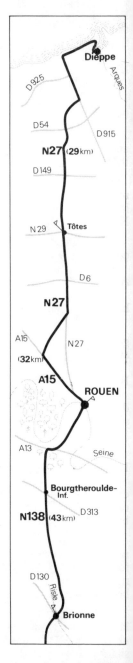

Fork right in the square, cross the River Risle and then the canal before climbing out of the valley and the town.

BERNAY
19th-century Folk Museum.

Again to cross Bernay, drop into and out of the valley.

Turn left at the lights at the bottom of the hill and then drive through the main street following the N138 for ALENÇON.

The N138 is a fine straight road which only permits itself minor twists and turns to negotiate villages such as Broglie and Gacé before crossing the N26.

Bypassing Sées, the road then sweeps into Alençon.

ALENÇON
Famous lace museum in the hôtel de ville (town hall).

The city has no true bypass but there is a very good inner ring road. Simply follow the signs for LE MANS, still on the N138.

BEAUMONT-SUR-SARTHE
Ownership of this pleasant old town was hotly disputed by those on both sides of the Channel on several occasions.

Your road passes straight through.

LE MANS
Famous for its 24-hour motor race. Three such events are now held each year — the two additional races being for motorcycles and, would you believe, heavy lorries.

Approaching the town, you pass under the motorway Paris — Rennes. Then watch carefully for the green sign, AUTRES DIRECTIONS, which is a right-hand turn onto the bypass which has not yet been completed.

Approaching traffic lights, take the left-hand lane. Follow it through the lights onto a roundabout and sweep round to the left following the sign for AUTRES DIRECTIONS.

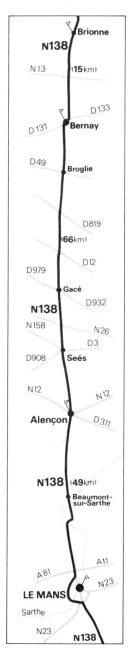

Continue onto the dual carriageway and cross the River Sarthe. Then cross the railway, watching for green signs to TOURS.

Watch for a flyover (Pont d'Auto) which crosses over your path. It is a good landmark and immediately you pass under it, take the right-hand filter lane signed TOURS.

You are now heading south on the N138.

As you leave the outskirts of the town, you travel for several miles on part of the Le Mans motor racing circuit. This is easy to pick out by the armoured crash barriers on both sides of the road.

The next village you will encounter is Mulsanne and, until you reach it, you are, in fact, driving on the Mulsanne Straight.

ECOMMOY

The N138 runs straight through this small town with its tree-lined streets.

The good two-lane road runs through avenues of trees and there are plenty of picnic spots.

TOURS

In our opinion, Tours is one of the most beautiful and certainly the best kept, tidiest city in France. It really enjoys the benefits of its two lovely rivers, the Loire and the Cher, to the full.

Entering Tours, turn left immediately before the first river bridge. This will take you along the bank of the Loire which is on your right.

Watch for the AUTRES DIRECTIONS sign which will swing you to the right, up a slip road and across the next bridge over the river.

Immediately after the river bridge, turn left. The Loire is now on your left, but only for 183m/200yds before you turn right.

The inner ring road then takes you to the south of the city, to a rather complicated junction where you must watch carefully for signs to POITIERS, which lead you onto the N10.

From Tours to Poitiers, the N10 is mostly a wide three-lane, two-way road with a good surface.

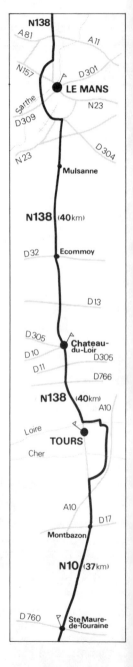

STE-MAURE-DE-TOURAINE

Renowned for its goats' cheese. The town has some quite useful hotels on the main road.

Follow the N10 straight through the town.

CHÂTELLERAULT

Well-known for the manufacture of quality cutlery.

At the approach to the town, watch for the sign to POITIERS. You swing right onto a pretty good inner ring road bypass. Simply follow the signs for POITIERS.

The N10 runs on south to Poitiers.

This route ends at Poitiers. Which road you take through the city will depend very much on your eventual destination.

For Bordeaux and Biarritz, you should turn to Route Fourteen (see page 99).

For Limoges, Toulouse, Narbonne and the Mediterranean, turn to Route Fifteen. (see page 102.)

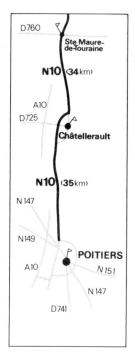

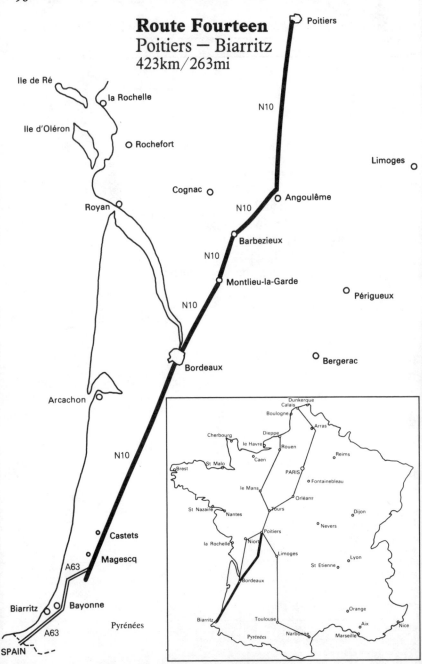

Route Fourteen
Poitiers — Biarritz
423km/263mi

Route Fourteen   Poitiers — Biarritz

This route starts as you approach Poitiers, travelling south on the N10. You will probably have arrived at this point by following Route Thirteen.

POITIERS

We suggest you leave the N10 just before Poitiers and bypass the city by motorway on the A10 at the junction for Poitiers-Nord. Watching for the blue motorway signs, before you reach Poitiers, which read NIORT and BORDEAUX.

Travel on the motorway for only 12km/7½mi to the junction for Poitiers-Sud. Leave the autoroute and rejoin the N10 (signs for ANGOULÊME and BORDEAUX).

The N10 at this point is a two-way, two-lane road, typical of a French N road. Throughout the distance from Poitiers to Angoulême, the N10 bypasses all the small towns and villages of any consequence.

ANGOULÊME

Proud of its reputation in the manufacture of high-quality paper, the town is also well known for making felt slippers and light-weight shoes. The city ramparts are well worth a visit.

There is an excellent bypass. Just follow green signs for BORDEAUX and continue on the N10.

BARBEZIEUX

Well-known for its marron glacé and even more famous for its Cognac, which is offered for sale at every small farm along the roadside.

Follow the N10 straight through this pretty little town.

MONTLIEU-LA-GARDE

The N10 goes straight through this small town at the northern edge of the Bordeaux wine region.

BORDEAUX

Important centre of the Bordeaux wines and capital of south west France and the Atlantic coast. It also has a busy and thriving port. The city is justifiably proud of its elegant buildings matched only in Paris.

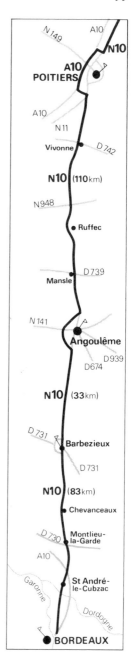

BORDEAUX BYPASS

Bordeaux has an excellent bypass — but it is important to pass on the western side of the city and not the eastern. After crossing the bridge over the River Dordogne, watch for signs to BAYONNE.

This will lead you onto the superb bypass and across the spectacular bridge over the Garonne which is even more impressive when crossed from the south heading north. The bypass circumnavigates the city through a series of junctions, each numbered rather like the exits from a British motorway. For example, those heading for the famous wine chateaux take junction no. 7 Médoc. We go on until we see junction no. 15 BAYONNE/SAN SEBASTIAN.

There are no tolls to pay on the stretch of motorway leading south from Bordeaux. It changes to dual carriageway of almost motorway standard as it reverts to being the N10 and enters the vast forests of the Gironde.

The road continues to be of a very high standard but the forests which, at first, seem fascinating become boring as they continue for approximately 80km/50mi. If you are taking a break — there are lovely picnic spots — you might be interested to note that many of the trees are tapped to collect resin, rather as rubber is collected in the tropics.

CASTETS

The N10 bypasses this quiet little town and then sweeps by Magescq in a similar manner.

Soon after, you will reach the entrance to the A63 autoroute. We recommend taking this motorway to bypass Bayonne. It involves payment of a toll but is well worth the money spent.

If you are intending to head on into Spain you would be well advised to select your onward routes before reaching Bayonne.

The A63 motorway sweeps past Bayonne through woods and sand dunes and crosses the magnificent River Adour to bring you right to the outskirts of Biarritz at motorway junction no. 4.

When heading for the Pyrénées or intending to cross France towards the Mediterranean you should leave the motorway at junction no. 6 and follow signs for PAU.

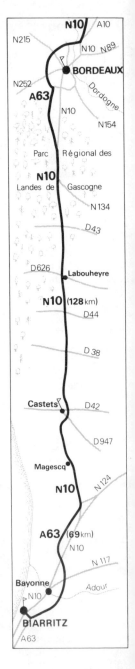

Route Sixteen
Poitiers — Narbonne
605km/375mi

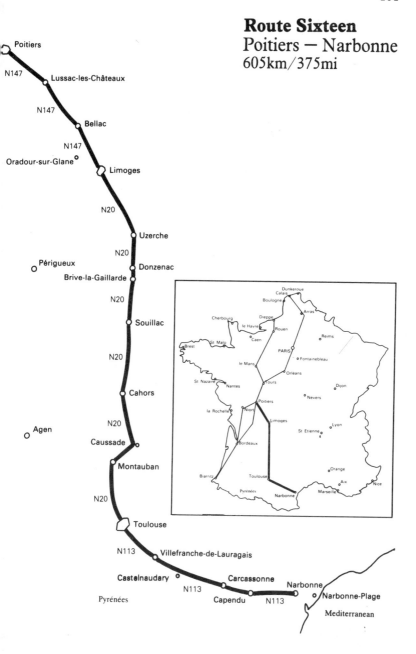

Poitiers

N147

Lussac-les-Châteaux

N147

Bellac

N147

Oradour-sur-Glane

Limoges

N20

Uzerche

N20

Périgueux

Donzenac

Brive-la-Gaillarde

N20

Souillac

N20

Cahors

N20

Agen

Caussade

Montauban

N20

Toulouse

N113

Villefranche-de-Lauragais

Castelnaudary

N113

Carcassonne

Narbonne

Capendu

N113

Narbonne-Plage

Pyrénées

Mediterranean

Route Sixteen   Poitiers — Narbonne

This route starts as you are approaching Poitiers, travelling south on the N10. You will probably have reached this point by following our Route Thirteen.

POITIERS
Just north of the city you will pass the motorway junction. Do not be tempted to take the motorway to bypass Poitiers as it is of no advantage when heading for Limoges.

Continue straight ahead towards the centre of Poitiers.

As you approach the city, the river is on your left and a high escarpment of rocks is to your right. At the first main junction, take the left-hand lane which takes you left (signed LIMOGES) under the railway bridge.

Go straight ahead, keeping just to the right of the column or tower in the middle of the road.

In the park which follows, there is a flyover bridge and as soon as you pass under it, turn left. This takes you up a slip road onto a first-class bypass high above the town which feeds direct onto the N147 for LIMOGES.

LUSSAC-LES-CHÂTEAUX
The N147 climbs and winds into the town with its tree-lined square.

BELLAC
Birthplace of playwright Jean Giraudoux 1882—1944 to whom there is a memorial.

Drive straight through, over the railway and straight ahead on the N147.

Those not in a hurry might consider leaving the N147 between Bellac and Limoges (just north of Chamboret) to visit the village of Oradour-sur-Glane which was completely destroyed by the Germans on 10 June, 1944 and all the inhabitants of the village, including 247 children, were executed in the most brutal way. The village is preserved just as the Nazis left it. It is the most moving memorial to human suffering that we have ever encountered.

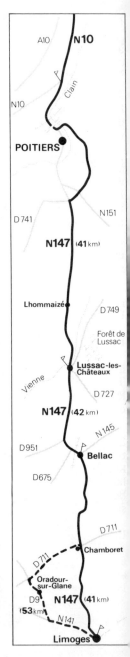

LIMOGES

Centre of the manufacture of china, porcelain and enamels. The very impressive Gothic cathedral took over 300 years to construct.

The N147 winds steeply uphill to enter the city. At the top of the hill, turn right following the sign for TOULOUSE. You pass the famous Limousin Stadium on your right as you follow onto the dual carriageway of the inner ring road.

Watch for the beautiful bridges over the River Vienne. You pass under the stone arches of the railway bridge and then turn right, over the second bridge, signed BRIVE and TOULOUSE. Continue out of town on the dual carriageway, watching carefully for a left hand turn signed TOULOUSE.

Then continue straight ahead, be careful not to be drawn into the industrial estate which lies on your right, then turn right onto the N20 signed TOULOUSE.

The N20 is a very good dual carriageway which remains a good road as it slips down towards Uzerche.

UZERCHE

You pass through a tunnel on the way into this ancient town. Drive straight on up a steep climb. The picturesque old town lies on your right as you leave. Follow the N20 straight on in the direction of BRIVE.

South of Uzerche, the N20 varies in quality. Sometimes it is a fast dual carriageway and sometimes an inferior N road. Watch for the signs BRIVE PAR DONZENAC and BRIVE DIRECT— the latter is a very good dual carriageway. Now you begin to see more interesting views of the countryside ahead.

BRIVE-LA-GAILLARDE

Centre of a market gardening region, producing a vast range of vegetables which are distributed to all the major cities of France, including far-away Paris.

There is no real bypass and the through route is very badly signed. To make it even more confusing

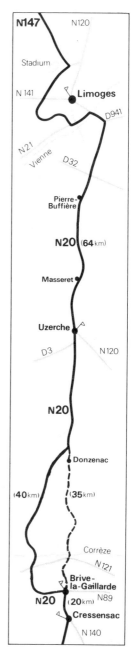

the signs for CAHORS and TOULOUSE change colour at almost every junction. Take great care concentrating on road signs and with a little luck and patience you will soon be on the N20 again, heading south.

SOUILLAC
Before entering the town, you descend the long, winding slopes of tree-covered hills that go down to the valley of the Dordogne.

Pass straight through the lively little town of Souillac with its beautiful abbey, over the River Dordogne and then prepare to climb to the extensive plateau beyond.

The road twists and winds over the hills, through scenery reminiscent of the Forest of Dean.

Follow the signs for CAHORS and we suggest you avoid the route signed Cahors Touristique unless you have a lot of time to spare.

CAHORS
As you descend towards Cahors, there are superb views of the valley and the River Lot. Cahors is famous for its rich, red, almost black wine. It is the birthplace of 19th-century politician Léon Gambetta. The impressive city ramparts date back to the 13th and 14th centuries.

Negotiate the town with care, always watching for the N20 signs to MONTAUBAN.

The N20, south of Cahors, has many small roadside hotels offering very good accommodation at most reasonable prices.

CAUSSADE
A very good bypass rushes you past this little market town. Just follow the green signs for TOULOUSE.

The N20 is very straight and well-surfaced as it heads on south towards Montauban.

MONTAUBAN
Seven brick arches of the 14th-century bridge link the old town to the more modern suburbs.

There is no true bypass but the town centre can be avoided by carefully following an intricate but well-signed route through the suburbs. Follow signs for TOULOUSE.

TOULOUSE
Home of the French aircraft industry, this brick-built city has produced the Caravelle, Mirage and Concorde. It is the fourth largest city in France but crossing it from north to south is quite simple if care is taken when picking out direction signs.

Approaching the city, you drive through miles of industrial estates until you come upon the blue motorway signs for MONTPELLIER. This will lead onto what is, in fact, not really motorway but a very good dual carriageway, which crosses the River Garonne by an impressive bridge. Continue to follow the blue MONTPELLIER signs.

You come to a very large roundabout controlled by traffic lights. Pass under the flyover and turn right, beside the railway. You cross the Garonne twice more, all the time following the blue signs for MONTPELLIER. Then pick up green signs for CARCASSONNE on the N113.

The N113 from Toulouse to Carcassonne, which runs parallel to the A61 motorway, undulates through gentle countryside as it follows the path of the Canal du Midi. The canal is now almost exclusively the domain of pleasure craft although it was constructed as an important industrial link between the Mediterranean and the Atlantic. Looking from the N113 to the right, there are really beautiful views of the majestic Pyrénées.

VILLEFRANCHE-DE-LAURAGAIS
A right-hand fork as you enter the town is all that is necessary to bypass it and lead you on towards Narbonne.

CASTELNAUDARY
The important canal basin in the town makes it an automatic centre for pleasure boats. The recipe for the rich stew, cassoulet is said to have originated here.

The main road bypasses the town and you are hardly aware of its existence as you pass by.

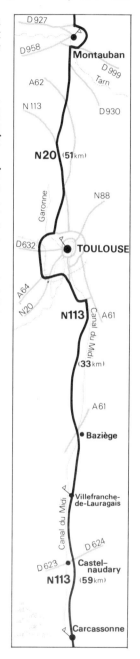

CARCASSONNE

The town is dominated by the ancient fortress known as La Cité which is recognised as the finest surviving medieval fortification in the world.

Traffic usually flows easily through Carcassonne. Simply pursue the signs which clearly mark the route to NARBONNE.

The N113 continues to run roughly parallel to the A61 motorway. The route now passes through a sub-tropical region which clearly indicates that the Mediterranean is not far ahead.

CAPENDU

There are splendid views of the Château Capendu as you pass easily through this sleepy little town.

This area is one of the most prolific producers of wine in France. The vineyards of Corbières produce superb table wines (vins de table).

The N113 runs straight ahead into Narbonne and as the D168 on to Narbonne-Plage.

Those heading on into Spain, the Pyrénées or towards the Côte d'Azur will find it easy to pick up the A9 motorway without entering Narbonne.

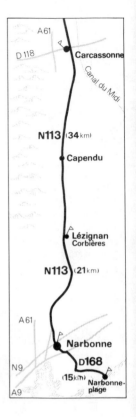

Route Sixteen
Calais — Bordeaux by motorway
877km/544mi

Route Sixteen Calais — Bordeaux by motorway

FOR CALAIS — PARIS (N1), see pages 46—47, Route One. The fast route to Paris by the A26 and A1 autoroutes can be followed in Route Twelve. See page 89.

FOR PARIS — THE RING ROAD see pages 49—50, Route Two.

Heading south out of Paris, it is very easy to pick up blue motorway signs for ORLÉANS, the first major town on the A10 motorway.

There is a toll barrier 64km/40mi from Paris, immediately after which the A10 motorway divides with the A11 leading to Le Mans and Central Brittany. We take the lane clearly signed for the A10 to ORLÉANS.

The first 120km/75mi of the A10 motorway to Orléans tends to be fairly heavily congested, a condition now common to most motorways feeding major cities. Once south of Orléans and heading for TOURS, the flow of traffic improves quite dramatically. Driving becomes a real pleasure and this is indeed a true urban freeway. Free but for the never-ending reminders that you are paying heavy tolls for your freedom of progress.

As you head south towards Tours, there is a pronounced change of scenery with the fertile Île-de-France giving way to the rolling hills and dairy lands of the centre of France.

The A10 motorway which sweeps on south is well-surfaced but it is exposed to crosswinds in places. It is no more interesting than any other motorway. Services are infrequent and, in our opinion, expensive.

As well as being a very fast route from Paris to Bordeaux, the motorway also forms the north to south bypass for Châtellerault, Poitiers, Niort and Saintes before crossing the Dordogne to run easily into the Bordeaux bypass system. See page 100, Route Fourteen.

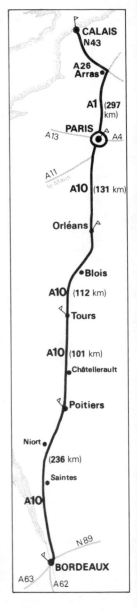

Route Seventeen
Dieppe — Brest, Normandy and Brittany
554km/337mi

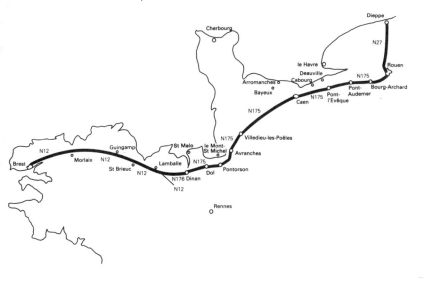

Route Seventeen   To Normandy,
North Britanny   Dieppe — Brest

If you are aiming to drive deep into Britanny, you have a wide choice of ferry crossings available to you. Some motorists may prefer to take the short crossing to Calais or Boulogne, in which case they can link into the Britanny route at Rouen, following Route Four. Those crossing to Le Havre, St Malo or Cherbourg will head south for only a few miles until they join up with us. When visiting Britanny, we prefer the ferry crossing from Newhaven to Dieppe simply because it sails right into the heart of a French town — and we find that exciting.

DIEPPE

Dieppe claims to be the oldest seaside resort in France.

Ferries docking at Dieppe tie up in a pool right in the centre of the old town itself. It is a very impressive first look into the everyday life of France.

When you drive from the ferry, following the quay to customs and passport control, you pass from the town centre to emerge onto the French roads along the esplanade which fronts the sea.

Drive straight ahead for the full length of the sea front. At the far end, the road turns sharp left under the walls of the castle dominating the cliff in front of you. Follow signs for PARIS — ROUEN.

Go straight ahead past the traffic lights, continuing up the hill.

Watch for the fork to Paris and Rouen. You require the right fork for ROUEN. Follow the N27.

At a point 16km/10mi before Rouen, you have the choice of continuing on the N27 or taking the motorway. Take the motorway: it is toll-free, and you will enter Rouen by a much easier route.

ROUEN

This is a merchant shipping port even though it lies some 64km/40mi inland on the Seine. Rouen is a town of churches and museums. There are over 700 half-timbered houses.

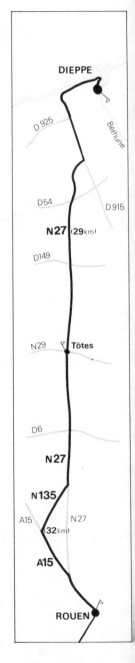

When the motorway ends, you will find yourself almost immediately onto the cobbles of the dock area. Follow the green overhead signs indicating TOUTES DIRECTIONS.

The next overhead sign is blue to PARIS. Follow it up the slip road which then swings right, over the Seine bridge.

From the bridge, the route goes straight ahead until just south of the city where you will see the sign for CAEN.

From this point to Caen, you have the choice of using either the N175 or the A13 motorway. Unless you are in a desperate hurry, we suggest that you travel on the N175 by following the A13 through wooded land to a point where you can fork to the right onto the N175, signed for Caen. The road passes through some quite lovely little towns and villages.

BOURG-ACHARD
A pleasant little town. Nearby, there are superb views of the valley of the Seine. You can watch ships negotiating the meanders of the river from vantage points high above it.

PONT-AUDEMER
Centre of the tanning industry. The eastern half of the town has a bypass which at first appears as though it will sweep you right past the town. Unfortunately it is not yet complete. At the end of the bypass just follow signs for CAEN.

THE NORMANDY BEACHES (Detour)
Many visitors to this part of France will be drawn to the beachheads where the Allied Forces landed on 6 June, 1944.

The beaches with code names, *Sword, Juno, Gold, Omaha* and *Utah,* span some 80km/50mi between Cabourg (Pegasus Bridge) and the Cherbourg peninsula. Probably the most interesting place to visit is the quiet little town of Arromanches from where you can view clearly the large sections of the Mulberry Harbour which have survived more than forty years of pounding by the angry seas. In the town itself, you can inspect tanks, guns and landing craft dating back to D-Day.

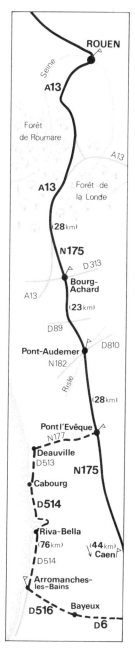

The museum on the front is well worth visiting. We were quite surprised by the remarkable detail of many of the models on display.

Those intending to visit the beaches should leave the N175 before Caen and rejoin it afterwards: turn north at Pont-l'Évèque to DEAUVILLE and then follow the beaches as far as Arromanches — further if you wish. To return to the N175, travel by way of Bayeux and then follow the D6 signs until the road joins the N175.

CAEN

University city and capital of lower Normandy. Two-thirds of the city was destroyed in the fighting that followed the Normandy landings in 1944. The rebuilding programme has been most successful and the 19th-century canal has been improved to take ships of 5000 tons to a point some 16km/10mi inland where they are loaded and discharged.

Before reaching Caen, you will come to a junction where large green signs show TOUTES DIRECTIONS to your left.

Turn left. Cross over the motorway, following signs to CAEN SUD.

Follow the signs for PÉRIPHÉRIQUE SUD. When you reach a junction where Alençon is signed to your left, you must turn right as if heading into Caen.

Turn left at the green overhead signs showing LAVAL, CHERBOURG and RENNES. You now travel straight through a residential area where there are large blocks of flats.

At the traffic lights, Laval and Flers are signed to the left — you turn right. Follow the TOUTES DIRECTIONS signs.

Pick up signs for AVRANCHES and ST MICHEL.

VILLEDIEU-LES-POÊLES

Known as the copper city Villedieu-les-poêles is proud of its copperware museum and its bell foundry. Hand-beaten copper plate is still worked in the town.

The N175 forks left to bypass this sleepy little market town.

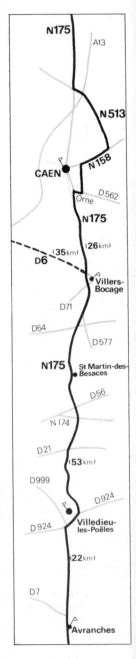

AVRANCHES

As you approach Avranches, known as the city of flowers, the impressive silhouette of the church dominates the skyline. This was the site of General Patton's headquarters in 1944. On clear days there are fine views of Mont-St-Michel from the botanic gardens.

Follow green signs for MONT-ST-MICHEL. Cross over the bridge, watching for the right-hand turn and then Avranches is behind you.

PONTORSON

Sitting on the boundary between Normandy and Brittany, this little village is the gateway to Mont-St-Michel.

LE MONT-ST-MICHEL (Detour)

We feel that almost everyone passing this way will wish to deviate from their route at Pontorson to drive the 8km/5mi down to the coast where the sight of Mont-St-Michel is quite breathtaking.

The 11th-century abbey stands on top of a rock which rises 155m/500ft from the sandy beach. The granite mount also supports a small town, complete with cafés and souvenir shops. It is connected to the mainland by a long causeway over the sands.

Continue on the N176 to Dol.

DOL-DE-BRETAGNE

Looking seaward from Dol, you can see columns of rock which are so typical of this area.

ST MALO (Detour)

This historic town was almost completely destroyed in World War Two but it has been restored in a manner that makes it difficult to believe that it mostly consists of very modern buildings.

The E.D.F. (Électricité de France) have built a tidal control barrage across the estuary of the Rance and it is well worth a visit. Constructed in the sixties, this is man's first attempt to harness the tide and use its power to generate electricity.

Many will feel it to be well worth leaving the direct route to visit St Malo. Turn right onto the

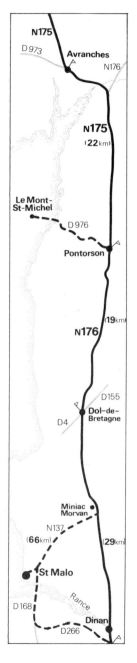

N137 signed ST MALO. When returning, cross the highway built on the Barrage du Rance and watch carefully for the left turn to DINAN.

DINAN

The Route Nationale which has now become the N176 enters the town over a stone viaduct which offers elevated views of the old port far below – now a marina for pleasure boats. The road climbs past the ancient château into the cobbled square of this delightful town. The motor museum is well worth a visit.

Your road, clearly signed for ST BRIEUC, goes straight through the town centre, joining the new road from St Malo at a very complicated junction near the aerodrome on the far side of town. Watch carefully for green signs to ST BRIEUC.

LAMBALLE

Just before Lamballe, the N176 joins the N12 from Paris and the road improves quite dramatically from here onwards. Here the N12 is a dual carriageway of almost motorway standard without tolls, which bypasses Lamballe.

ST BRIEUC

This is the gateway to the Emerald Coast. There are fine views of the sea and the port from the dual carriageway which bypasses the town.

GUINGAMP

Famous for its July religious festivals which culminate each evening in candlelight processions as pilgrims, many in National dress, wend their way through the streets.

The dual carriageway enables you to bypass the town easily.

MORLAIX

Those who choose to stay on the main road, easily bypassing the town, will be treated to fine views of the railway viaduct to their left. This quite remarkable bridge is two-storey with the level-crossing raised high above the lower bridge.

Now the end of the Finistère Peninsula lies only 56km/35mi ahead. The N12 road is a very fine dual carriageway throughout the distance.

BREST

The Granite City that was almost completely destroyed in World War Two. Night after night, the allies blasted the city with multi-bomber raids in a fruitless attempt to destroy the German submarine pens which still survive and are used today by the French Navy.

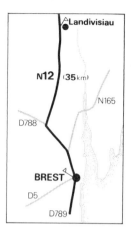

The main bridge over the port is the largest single-span, straight-lift bridge in the world.

The fine dual carriageway on which you crossed northern Brittany continues in a complete circuit of the Finistère Peninsula. Those following it to Quimper, Lorient, Vannes and passing St Nazaire to Nantes can be assured of good roads and an easy passage.

Route Eighteen
Dunkerque — la Rochelle
705km/437mi

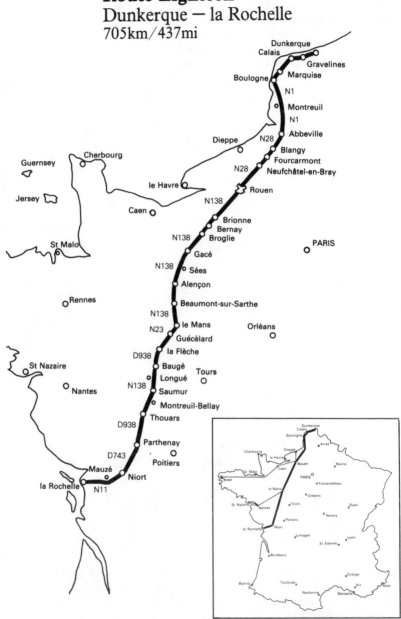

Route Eighteen

Dunkerque — La Rochelle

Facilities offered to ferry passengers at Dunkerque are poor and not very agreeable but if you find it more convenient to start your journey through France from here, take the following route through the port: leaving the landing area, you drive through a series of right-angle left and right bends across a wilderness of flat terrain to emerge onto the RN1 south of the town of Dunkerque. At the RN1, turn right, following signs towards CALAIS.

GRAVELINES
The N1 now bypasses this rather sad little town with its ancient port which survives by its meagre timber imports.

CALAIS
The major passenger port of France. Heading south into the town, it is easy to pick up the new bypass road which involves a left-hand turn at the traffic lights. Watch for signs to BOULOGNE.

MARQUISE
Follow the N1 through this straggly little town, famous for its marble quarries.

BOULOGNE
The 34km/21mi of uninteresting road from Calais or the 76km/45mi from Dunkerque to Boulogne can be avoided by taking a ferry directly from Dover to Boulogne at no extra cost.

Leaving Boulogne, watch for signs to PARIS and ABBEVILLE N1. Be careful not to take the road to Le Touquet.

From Boulogne, we follow the N1 on south through the vast wheat fields and root crops which are the mainstay of agriculture in northern France. Avenues of trees take the road ahead into the distant rolling hills.

MONTREUIL
Continue to follow the N1 which bypasses the

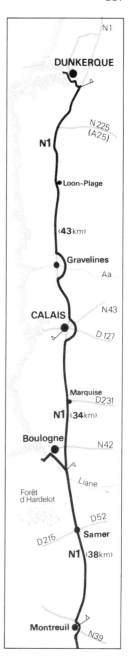

ancient town of Montreuil-sur-Mer with its cobbled streets. Head straight on down the N1, still following signs for ABBEVILLE.

ABBEVILLE
Dropping down the hill into Abbeville, it is a simple matter to spot the signs for ROUEN. Bear to the
right at the first roundabout onto a short stretch of
the new bypass.

Follow the canal which is lined with beautiful
poplar trees. After 1km/½mi turn right onto the
N28 towards ROUEN.

The N28 is a good road — very straight and
surely the way the Romans came to Britain.

The road at one point twists down into the pretty
little town of Blangy and then climbs again. In the
small town of Foucarmont, watch for a sharp turn
to the right which you come upon very suddenly.
The N28 continues very straight to Neufchâtel
through wooded hills. Follow signs N28 towards
ROUEN.

ROUEN
There are magnificent views of the city sprawled
in your path as you descend on the N28. Do not be
tempted to follow the blue motorway signs that go
left towards Paris. Continue straight ahead following green TOUTES DIRECTIONS signs.

This will lead you through the inner ring road to
the point where you cross the bridge over the Seine
and you can see the vast inland port below on your
right.

Your route goes straight ahead from the bridge
until, south of the city, you take the right slip road
onto the N138 signed for ALENÇON.

BRIONNE
The road winds its way downhill into the town.
Fork right in the square, cross the River Risle and
then the canal before climbing out of the valley and
the town.

BERNAY
Again, you drop into and out of the valley to
cross Bernay, site of a 19th-century folk museum.

Turn left at the lights at the bottom of the hill.

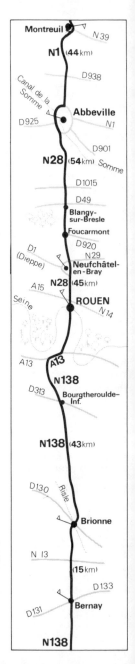

Then go through the main street, following the N138 for ALENÇON.

The N138 is a fine straight road which permits itself only minor twists and turns, to negotiate villages such as Broglie and Gacé before it crosses the N26.

After bypassing Sées, the road sweeps into Alençon.

ALENÇON
Famous lace museum in the town hall.

The city has no true bypass but there is a very good inner ring road. Simply follow the signs for LE MANS still on the N138.

BEAUMONT-SUR-SARTHE
A pleasant old town, ownership of which was the subject of dispute between those on both sides of the Channel on several occasions.

Your road passes straight through.

LE MANS
Famous for its 24-hour motor race. Three such events are now held annually. The two additional races are for motorcycles and, would you believe, heavy lorries.

Approaching the town, you pass under the motorway Paris — Rennes. Then watch carefully for the green signs for AUTRES DIRECTIONS, which is a right-hand turn onto the not yet complete bypass.

Take the left-hand lane at the next roundabout and turn left at the traffic lights following the sign for AUTRES DIRECTIONS.

Continue on the dual carriageway. Cross the River Sarthe and then watch carefully for the right-hand turn to ANGERS and SAUMUR. (The D147 leads onto the N23).

GUÉCÉLARD
The main road passes straight through this busy little town.

Just after Guécélard, the Hercule Buckmaster memorial to the French Resistance movement is close beside the N23 on your left.

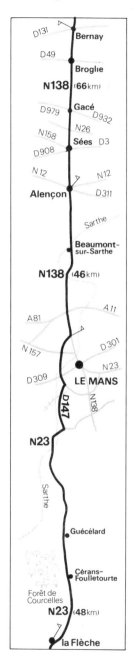

LA FLÈCHE

An avenue of trees leads to a roundabout on the approach to the town. Turn left at the sign for SAUMUR and then right at the traffic lights. Turn left again 274m/300yds later onto the D308 — which for no apparent reason later becomes the D938.

BAUGÉ

Follow the green AUTRES DIRECTIONS signs and watch for the left turn to SAUMUR at the traffic lights. Then take a right turn off a very tight round-about which takes you up the hill on the D938 towards SAUMUR.

LONGUÉ

You can bypass Longué without being aware of it, and pick up the N138. (Some older road signs remain which show the N138 to be the N147 — just ignore them.)

The countryside is flat as you cross into the Loire Valley on the approaches to Saumur.

SAUMUR

Famous for its méthode champenoise sparkling wines. As you approach the town, there are points where you are treated to a momentary glimpse of the 14th-century château.

The through-route takes you sharp right, just before the river, signed NIORT. Then you swing to the left to cross the river. The road runs to the left again, past the cavalry school, before you turn right at traffic lights to cross the River Thouet.

After the river-crossing, the N138 again tries to masquerade as the N147 as it goes long and straight towards MONTREUIL-BELLAY.

MONTREUIL-BELLAY

This lovely old fortified town has a very good bypass. Follow the signs for THOUARS.

The same main road continues south, having decided to call itself the D938!

THOUARS

The route through the town is tortuous and requires a high degree of concentration. (A bypass is promised.) Just follow signs for PARTHENAY and NIORT.

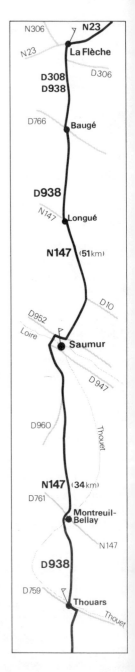

PARTHENAY

One of the largest weekly cattle markets in France.

Cross the narrow bridge and climb up the road to the town, which is straight ahead. At the round-about, care is necessary in selecting the route signed NIORT.

The D743 from Parthenay to Niort is an excellent road, through beautiful countryside.

NIORT

There are three separate routes, signed throughout the town, to LA ROCHELLE. It does not matter which one you take but we prefer CENTRE VILLE. The streets of the town are a little narrow in parts, but traffic flows well and the square at the heart of the town is most attractive.

MAUZÉ-SUR-LE-MIGNON

The N11 bypasses the town and then goes into a very strange, but modern junction where it divides into what most maps show as the N22 and D911.

In fact, the N22 has been rechristened as the N11 and is signed for LA ROCHELLE.

The N11 is a good road as it speeds you to the coast and right into the heart of La Rochelle, our favourite resort on the Atlantic coast.

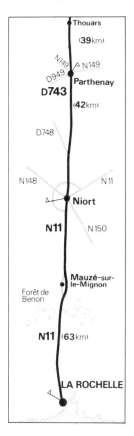

Route Nineteen
le Mans — St Nazaire
216km/134mi

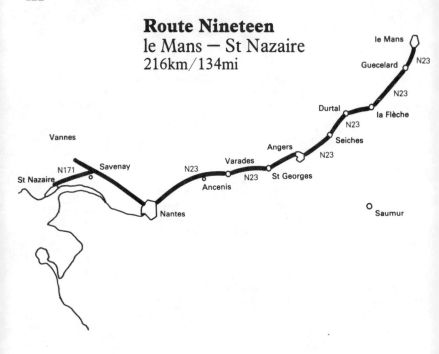

Route Nineteen   Le Mans — St Nazaire

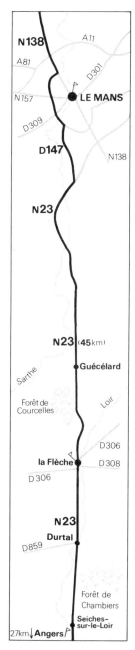

For Dieppe to Le Mans, see Route Thirteen, page 94. For Dunkerque, Calais or Boulogne to Le Mans, see Route Eighteen, page 117. You will be approaching the city travelling south on the N138.

LE MANS
Famous for its 24-hour motor race. Three such events are now held annually. The two additional races are for motorcycles and, would you believe, for heavy lorries.

Approaching the town, you pass under the motorway Paris — Rennes. Then watch carefully for the green signs indicating AUTRES DIRECTIONS which is a right-hand turn onto the not yet complete bypass.

Approaching from the left-hand lane, take the left-hand turn, signed AUTRES DIRECTIONS, at the traffic lights by the roundabout.

Continue on the dual carriageway, crossing the River Sarthe. Then watch carefully for the right-hand turn to ANGERS and SAUMUR. (The D147 leads onto the N23.)

GUÉCÉLARD
The main road passes straight through this busy little town.

Just after Guécélard, the Hercule Buckmaster memorial to the French Resistance movement is close beside the N23 on your left.

LA FLÈCHE
Follow the N23 straight through the town. Watch for the twin châteaux standing each side of the Loir.

DURTAL
A very congested little town. The main street was not designed for modern-day traffic.

The N23 is a pleasant road, passing through orchards and fruit farms.

SEICHES-SUR-LE-LOIR
The main road easily passes straight through this small town.

ANGERS

Famous for its rosé wines.

Just 185m/200yds after the N23 enters the city limits, there is a right-hand turn signed NANTES — RENNES — LAVAL. Take it.

This leads through the suburbs until it swings you left along the bank of the river.

Pass the château on your left and cross the river, following green overhead signs for NANTES.

As the N23 runs out into the countryside, watch carefully for the beautiful Château de Serrant on your left, some 16km/10mi out of Angers.

ST GEORGES-SUR-LOIRE

You can drive straight through this pretty little town with its lovely old windmill.

VARADES

Travelling straight through the town, from the N23, you catch an occasional glimpse of the Loire or a distant château.

ANCENIS

The first Breton town on the Loire, it is a little more lively on market day.

Follow the main road through the outskirts of this little market town.

NANTES

Although 60km/37mi from the open sea, it is one of the most important ports in France. Nantes was the centre of the slave trade until its abolition, since when the city has continued to be one of the most prosperous trade centres in France.

Nantes is the seventh largest city in France and is devoted to gastronomy with a tradition of dining in some style. The local Gros Plant and Muscadet wines complement duck, chicken and fish served in a creamy butter sauce. Frogs legs are a further renowned speciality of the region.

Follow the N23 in towards the heart of the city until you see green signs to VANNES and RENNES which swing you to the right onto a dual carriage-way.

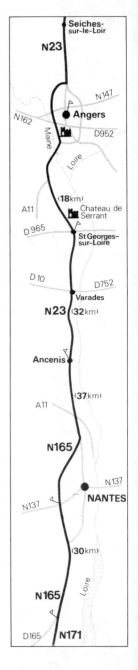

The bypass suffers from two or three quite complicated junctions but it is fairly easy to follow if you watch carefully for signs to VANNES.

You will emerge from the city on the N165 which is a good dual carriageway.

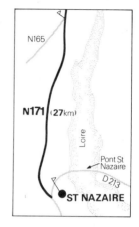

ST NAZAIRE

Some 24km/15mi ahead, in open country, lies the fork for St Nazaire. Take the N171. This junction is just before the town of Savenay which both roads bypass.

Soon you will have your first view of the incredible Pont St Nazaire. This bridge is, to our mind, one of the 'Seven Wonders of France', and is among the most awe-inspiring civil engineering feats we have encountered.

Index

All main entries are printed in heavy type. Route numbers and the abbreviation 'R. Nap.' (Route Napoléon) are also printed in heavy type. The route number precedes the page number.

128